Monster Eyes

KIMOTHY MONROE

Copyright © 2019 Kimothy Monroe
All rights reserved
First Edition

PAGE PUBLISHING, INC.
Conneaut Lake, PA

First originally published by Page Publishing 2019

ISBN 978-1-64544-962-1 (pbk)
ISBN 978-1-64701-253-3 (hc)
ISBN 978-1-64544-963-8 (digital)

Printed in the United States of America

PREFACE

This book is the first I have ever written, and I have never had the slightest desire to write a book. As far as reading a book goes, heck, I haven't read many books that I didn't stop halfway through just to never pick it up again and finish it. But when I became involved in such a gruesome and horrific ordeal that touched the lives of many, I was compelled to put it on paper and tell the world. This book is a real and nonfiction account of how people's lives can be changed in an instant. The names and locations in the book have been changed to protect the lives and privacy of the innocent. My book will allow the reader to get a look into the lives of real people, people we are supposed to put our trust in but sometimes and somehow fail us. It takes you into the mind of the psychotic, the mentally disturbed, and the sexual deviant who cries out with rage and anger to satisfy their own sick desires. People across the world have been touched by some type of crime or will be at some point in their lives. Some crimes are less severe than others, but for those who had tragedy and despair to strike in their lives, they will hopefully understand and appreciate what this book is all about. For those who haven't been touched by any travesties as of yet, I encourage you to read *Monster Eyes*. Beware and educate yourselves on how to handle unexpected events that may make you, your neighbor, or somebody you love the next victim.

    Even though I was not an actual victim of circumstance surrounding the graphic events outlined herein, I became a victim because it consumed me just about every day until the horrific ordeal came to a sudden end. But even after the end came, I, along with other citizens of this small town nestled in southeastern North Carolina, still felt victimized because we were held under siege for two years. During those years, we could see the faces of the ones we knew and loved, and those are the faces that will be etched in our hearts and minds forever.

People in small towns rarely experience what we had to endure, and because of that, nobody who lives in such a small population can ever be truly prepared. Preparations usually take place after tragedy strikes in most cases. Even after tragedy struck in our town, we still did not take precautions and prepare for the worst. The result was another vibrant and beautiful young woman who was most proud to be an educator in our public school system and who was stopped short in the pinnacle of her life. If you don't know how it feels to lose the only loved one you have, ask the families of Sallie Hatcher and Loretta Brodus.

Natural death is something we all know, expect, lament about, and eventually accept, but an intentional, vicious, and animalistic death is something that will haunt you forever. *Monster Eyes* is mainly dedicated to those families who have lost their loved ones to a tragic death at the hands of a killer. My heart truly goes out to those families, and I would simply say to all of you who read this book, to never forget your loved one, remember them, and cherish them. Make their memory a memorial, and make their death increase your will to live. Tell others about the goodness of the ones you lost, and let their goodness perpetuate and radiate every time you speak of them. I implore those in mourning to try your best to keep families together and keep them in love for the sake of the slain beloved. Families need to know how important it is to remain within the unit and not take anyone's existence for granted, not even for a day.

Life bears no promises and can expire on any given day. Most of us aren't prepared for the inevitable and the unexpected and never ask ourselves the question of what we would do if tragedy struck. Tell your friends and family you love them, and show them in special ways when time allows while you can. I dedicate *Monster Eyes* to my mother, Swanoria Monroe Hall, who lost her battle to cancer. Her death wasn't at the hands of a physical killer, but a silent and internal one that stole her from us in record time. My mom knew we loved her, and I told her often as she did me, and we will miss her deeply. This book is also dedicated to the families of Sallie Hatcher and Loretta Brodus. To them, I say thank you for allowing me to express my innermost thoughts on paper and share with the world what we have shared among ourselves. I also thank my true friends who have supported me, believed in me, and pushed me to finish *Monster Eyes*. I especially want to thank my wife Cherie for listening to my story, being patient with me, and sharing my story whenever she got the opportunity. She is special to me, and I appreciate the many nights she had to go to bed without me as I stayed up late at night banging on the computer keyboard in hopes of completing this book. Well, my love, the book is finished, and now we can go to bed together. I hope every reader enjoys the twists, perils, and the trials of *Monster Eyes* and always remember that somewhere, someone's eyes are watching you.

INTRODUCTION

It was the fall of 1980 when I was just a normal kid in college at North Carolina Central University in Durham, North Carolina. I was just beginning to find my way in life after two years of wondering which direction I would go and how I would get there. Most college minds learn to think big, inherit big egos, and have thoughts of commanding big salaries postgraduation. I was no different. I had big plans and found myself interested in the field of political science and criminal justice, and maybe even law school wasn't out of the question. I knew achieving the goals I set for myself would be hard because I am a product of a single-mother household where my mother wore both skirt and pants. She struggled to keep me and my siblings afloat and did a fine job with what she had to work with.

Our mother, Swanoria, or better known as Swan, worked very hard for many years as a nurse's aide at King's County Hospital in Brooklyn, New York. She had dreams like the rest of us to finish college and succeed in the medical profession. But with three fatherless children to take care of, her dreams were tossed aside, and she assumed the full-time role of mother and provider. As I remember, we lived in an apartment within the inner city known as Brownsville. Mom eventually felt the wave of violence creeping into the neighborhood and moved us to the Bushwick area and then to an even safer territory at the corner of Evergreen and Woodbine Street in Brooklyn. Our brownstone sat right next to a big beautiful Catholic church. The neighborhood was clean, quiet, and hosted a street full of working-class people. I was even allowed to go out on to the stoop and sometimes play on the concrete sidewalk, although I had to stay within calling distance of my mother at all times. I especially miss those times when the city would close all corridors to our street in the summer and hoist a big gigantic movie screen now known as Jumbotrons only yards from our brownstone. The screen would be set up in the middle of the street about six o'clock on Saturday evening. By seven o'clock, all our neighbors on the entire block would be sitting on stoops, lawn chairs, trash cans, and whatever else they could relax upon while we watched the latest movie of the month.

We were nurtured quite well by our mother, scolded when needed, and beaten when we needed it. I remember us coming home from school, which was only a block from our brownstone. Mom would sporadically check our arms, legs, and other parts of our bodies for track and needle marks. I used to think she was crazy for doing such a silly thing because I was so young. I knew and read about drugs, but I expected her to know us better than that because we never gave her any indication otherwise. But we had to play along, roll our sleeves up, and drop our pants. If we did not comply and humor her in her quest for what she called *track marks*, there would be great consequences to follow, specifically, a big black rubber strap across our asses. Now, I don't know where in the world she found that piece of rubber, but it surely hurt when she was forced to use it. I got the strap a few times but not as often as my sister Brendle. She was the middle child and the wild one out of our trio. My brother John, or better known as Teddy, was the oldest and the person in charge in my mother's absence.

It was fun growing up in New York, but just like Mom knew when it was time to leave Brownsville, she knew it was time to get us out of New York if we were going to survive and be productive. School-age kids were turning for the worst, drugs were becoming more prevalent, and violence escalated. She packed us up and moved us out of the big city to a small town of less than two thousand people. Wilson's Mills is the name of the town situated in the heart of Johnston County that is just a few miles east of Raleigh, the state's capital. It was the home and birthplace of my grandparents, Theodore and Merdia Durant.

Although I visited my grandparents during summer months, I never thought about living in this less-densely populated place on a permanent basis. People were different in a somewhat-carefree way. Kids my age were allowed to be out and about in the community without any parental supervision. They dressed different, and they oftentimes walked barefoot. I learned to conform to most things of southern culture, but walking with my bare feet was never something I could master. Every step I took on the hard dirt, gravel, and asphalt felt like walking on hot lava rock, so it didn't take me long to figure out that walking barefoot must be a southern thing, but it definitely wasn't for me.

My mother never gave me anymore than a couple of dollars a day while we lived in New York because she was afraid it would be taken by a bully, or I would use it to buy dope. The kids of Wilson's Mills had money in their pockets all the time because most of them made their own money by cropping tobacco on weekends and during the weekdays in the summer months. I tried that too because I wanted to make my own money as well, and I wanted my pockets to jingle like all the other kids. My mother eventually allowed me to accept a job offer to crop tobacco. What a joyous morning that was when I got up, put on some old dungarees, and got ready for a day's work. It appeared that it was going to be a great day. The day began at 5:00 AM when I jumped on the back of a faded yellow-and-white Chevy flatbed truck and rode to the local restaurant for a hearty breakfast with my buddies. We ate as much as we wanted, and all expenses were paid for by the round red faced farm owner who transported us named Burlough Honeywell. Then, it was off to work in the fields. Cropping seemed effortless to mostly everyone in the field and seemed no more than fun for me. Cropping at the beginning of my row of tobacco wasn't too bad. I still remember my cohorts as they passed me. They would crop the bottom of the stalk and sling the leaves under their arms as a spray of dirty water from the leaves showered my face. I actually thought they were toying with me until they all started passing me and slinging water, drenching me as they cropped. I still didn't think the work was all that bad until it began to get hot around 9:00 AM. I started sweating profusely, my back began to hurt from constantly bending over to crop the bottom of the stalk, and it seemed there was no end to the row I was assigned. I cropped several rows until the effects of the sun began to beat my entire body.

It was about eleven thirty when I literally passed out in the middle of the field from heat exhaustion. I thought Mr. Honeywell was a nice man initially until my buddies told him I passed out. As I awakened and found myself lying on my back in the dirt, I saw Mr. Honeywell's alter ego as he cursed at me and told me I wasn't shit, and I wasn't worth a damn. He took me home as I rode in the back of his flatbed, dropped me off, and never returned to pick me up again. Some things were better left alone to the natives, and cropping tobacco was one of those things. I never ever tried to enter another field again. Even though I never cropped tobacco again, I was eventually able to trade in my slacks for jeans. I stopped wearing suits on Sundays, allowed my PRO-Keds to get dirty, and traded my Coke bottle glasses for contacts. The town of Wilson's Mills slowly became my home.

Even though our matriarch of a mother took great care of us all, it was still not enough to achieve our dreams. As much as she wanted to provide more and often did, she wasn't able to do much more, even though she would have broken her back to get us to a better place in life. Therefore, I took odd jobs during school and during the summer months as a janitor for the local elementary school and as a tobacco bagger at a tobacco warehouse. As I grew older, I continued to get odd jobs at convenience stores and department stores, and I maintained those jobs until I graduated from Smithfield-Selma High School in the spring of 1980.

In the fall of that same year, I was accepted and attended North Carolina Central University in Durham, North Carolina, where I again struggled to make ends meet. It was even harder on my mother when I went to college because I took even more money from her already-strained pockets. But I lightened her load when I got a job driving school buses for Lowe's Grove Elementary, and I participated in a work-study program at the university to help pay for my tuition, books, and various other entities that came along with college life. I worked at a local pantry store on night shift where I would talk to the night-shift cops on patrol. I also provided transportation for hire for the chairman of the political science department, Dr. Ghoulum Choudhury. Driving Dr. Choudhury around was a great way to make much-needed cash. It was a good exchange between me and him because he didn't have a driver's license or a car, and I didn't have any money. My grades began to wane a little due to me working so much, but I had to prioritize. My priority was making more money so I could stay in school and not continue to burden my mother. Making more money didn't seem to help me totally meet my objective though, and I began to get involved in lots of nonscholastic and extracurricular activities. Older people call it "sowing my oats."

Eventually, the finances, the pressures, the socializing, and womanizing caught up with me, and I had to temporarily withdraw from school in order to get myself back together. I had to plan my next strategy as I had a baby on the way from my high school sweetheart, Connie Barnett who was also attending NCCU. I thought I had reached a point of emancipation and independence, which I worked hard to achieve, but it all came crashing down when I had to drop out of school and return home. I didn't know what I was going to do next, but I was fully aware that it was my mother who got me to college, and I was fully aware that it was I who must finish it.

CHAPTER 1

The Transition

I felt like a failure having to return home and depend on my mother again, but I knew in my mind it was only a reprieve. I had no real desire to live in Johnston County because the whole county seemed to be monopolized by the "good ole boys." Smithfield was famous back in those days as it was known across the country as the home of the KKK or better known as the Ku Klux Klan. The billboard advertising the KKK's existence stood tall at the entrance of the city limits near the center of town near the Neuse River bridge. Although time passed and times changed, many people who currently live in the area can still tell a story about that dreadful and intimidating sign. But it was home for me, and at the current time, I had no immediate plans of leaving.

I quickly picked up my old job at J. R. Tobacco Co. on Brogden Road. I remember that place being hot as hell and me working like a horse while sweat steadily rolled down my face and back until the end of the day when our shift was over. I never complained a whole lot while I worked there because the manager would always look out for me and provide me with employment every summer. When most high schoolers and college kids had to constantly and competitively look for jobs, I had one in the bag every year just for the asking. It was my third year in college when I had to withdraw and get a job to help ends meet. I had to make enough money to acquire certain things I needed, like a car, clothes, and child support for my daughter Kimbrel and a place for us to stay. Those kinds of things could not be supported by the tobacco-factory salary, and I sought a better-paying job with better benefits. I sought a different type of job not only to satisfy my financial burdens, but to give me more self-worth and to create a better me because I knew I had more to offer.

I saw an advertisement in the *Smithfield Herald* newspaper for a police officer. The salary was $11,000 a year with full major medical and dental benefits. The schedule was appealing as well, and it allowed me to be off every other weekend to at least enjoy my newfound adulthood. All that was required of me was to attend and pass a sixteen-week basic law enforcement training program, pass a physical, successfully complete a background investigation, and pass a probationary period of one year. I knew I would succeed on all levels and was very interested in applying for the job.

I never really noticed any black police officers in the area, so I had my doubts about the reception I would receive from a possibly racist and monopolized organization, but I maintained my confidence. I put on my best duds, which was my lucky blue suit and went to the Smithfield police station where I got an application, filled it out on the spot, and turned it in. Some people my age would have wondered how I could fill out such a lengthy application in one visit. Well, thanks to the little things learned in high school and college, I was well prepared with a résumé and a complete history of my background in hand, which made the application process easy. After turning in my application to a somewhat-nonchalant male person, I walked out not knowing if they would look at it or not, but little did I know, that day was the beginning of a new life for me.

The next day, I received a phone call from Joel Pearceton, the chief of police. I was really surprised, elated, baffled, grateful, scared, nervous, you name it, and the terminology would probably fit me when the call came in. He wanted to meet with me and talk more about the position and what we had to offer to each other. After several interviews, physicals, and rigorous training, I became a certified police officer for the town of Smithfield.

Never did I have intentions on staying in police work. I was eager to make some money, take care of some responsibilities I created, and return to school. But when I put on that dark navy-blue uniform with that big silver badge and those shiny patent-leather shoes, I was transformed into someone I never knew. I had a feeling of authority, class, and broad discretion when dealing with people's day-to-day problems. I actually had influence and impact on lives. I found myself actually enjoying something that I initially knew nothing about, and once I joined the force, it quickly became hard to part from the force because I became the force. It was fun, challenging, and interesting. Among a department of about thirtysomething employees, I was among only one other black officer whom I barely saw because we were on two totally opposite shifts. The division of the shift between he and me was intentional as well as strategical to give the false impression of representation. It was okay with us though because I got along with everyone at the department, and they made me feel like I was a part of what we call the blue-line brotherhood. Surprisingly though, not only did they make me feel a part of the organization, they showed me numerous times that I was a part of them. I even inherited the nickname Snowball. Connie Barnett and I eventually married, and we finally got a chance to provide a stable environment for our daughter. We all loved each other and had a great looking family, but Connie and I were still young, immature and trying to figure out life. We did figure it out, but unfortunately, it wasn't with each other. We divorced after three years but maintained a good working relationship.

After about two years, I did get my senses back together and snapped out of the blue euphoric aura I was in. I knew I had to finish college to prepare myself for the real world and for obstacles that may have come my way. Even though a lot of my counterparts did not have a degree, I was always told to go a step further than the rest in order to stand ahead and apart. A degree would put me in just that position, and I wanted it.

When I asked the chief if I could go back to school on a part-time basis, I was quickly told that time did not permit, and I was there to police and not be a student. I was turned down cold. But as the saying goes, when one door closes, another one opens.

During my second year with the force, I was casually approached by Sergeant McDonald from the Selma Police Department, which is literally the next town over from Smithfield. The sergeant invited me to work at his department and assured me it was a great place to work. I don't know why, but I believed every word Sergeant McDonald told me. After all, he had been working for Selma PD for many years already. Of course, I expressed my interest of returning to school to get my degree. Sergeant McDonald assured me it would not be a problem as we continued our conversation. He also promised a salary increase. It was too good to be true, but I took the chance anyway. Chief Pearceton reluctantly took and accepted my two-week resignation, and I subsequently became a police officer for the town of Selma.

CHAPTER 2

New Beginnings

I don't know why I was the chosen one, and I didn't waste a lot of time trying to find out. I was just happy to be there. I received a warm welcome from all the guys, and they gladly assisted me during my transition. I did find it a bit strange though. I was again the only other black officer that worked for the department. Sergeant McDonald was the first. I guess it shouldn't have been strange to me given the county I was still in. However, I couldn't help but sometimes feel alone and somewhat isolated in a white-male-dominated society because there was nobody to talk or bond with consistently. Whatever plight I had to deal with from a cultural point of view was not the same plight as my counterparts. Mac and I worked opposite shifts, but when I saw him during shift change, it was always a warm welcome. We eventually became friends on and off the job. Although he was older than I, he understood me, and I understood him. We could evaluate situations, address them, and resolve them just by our conversation. Our conversations were often deep, and a lot of our intimate thoughts about life and about the department were discussed among each other. However, our trust and respect for each other was never compromised.

Eventually, I even formed a very close relationship with a fellow officer named Charlie Bowman. Charlie was as white as white can get, but he was real, and we too understood each other. Only the two of us could laugh at black-and-white jokes and not be offended because we truly respected each other for who we were, and we were both proud of who we were. We accepted the fact we had folks within our race who were embarrassments, but we remained proud. We ate lunch together daily, and we even frequented each other's house from time to time where we would share laughs, have hearty meals, and talk shop. Charlie was a good guy who eventually rose through the rank to become chief of police.

All was going fine with me in Selma, and nobody ever showed me any hint of prejudice until the year of 1989 when I applied for sergeant after the current white sergeant retired. Things were going so well for me in Selma that I literally forgot where I was, and that was Johnston County, one of the most racist areas I have known. The day I applied for sergeant was just another day at the office for me, and I felt confident as ever. The day finally came when all applicants were called to the office to take the sergeant's exam. I was on time to take the test with pen and paper in hand. As I heard Chief Charlton Hickman say, "You can begin," I whipped my pen out and prepared to write but was stopped abruptly by the chief and was told I had to take the test in pencil. It was at that time my senses were alerted, and I realized what was happening, but I satisfied the requirement as we so often do in order to get to higher ground. I was the second among five other candidates to finish and felt real good about what I had splattered on paper. As I walked out the door, the chief gave me this unusual look as if to ask why I was there. I didn't fully understand that look, but then again, maybe I didn't want to understand it.

A couple of weeks passed without a word as to who the next sergeant would be. When I inquired about the results with the chief, he gave me a one-word answer and walked away, giving me a cold shoulder, which was definitely out of character for him. I asked him again about a week later and got the same response. Finally, I got a phone call to meet at the department one day during the week with all the other candidates to hear the announcement. The announcement was to inform everyone Charlie Bowman would be the next sergeant. I was totally bewildered and wondered how that could be. I had no problem with the test. I was knowledgeable about the questions on the test, and I had been at the police department quite some time before Charlie was hired. As a matter of fact, I was the one who convinced Charlie to leave Clayton PD and work for Selma because I, like Sergeant McDonald, thought Selma PD was a great place to work. A lot of emotions swirled my brain, but I didn't lose my composure. As I walked out of the room, the chief patted me on my shoulder and said, "I know how you feel." That pat confirmed everything I thought about the process. It was tainted from the beginning, and I never had a chance. I had never been so disappointed, saddened, and betrayed by someone I respected.

Racism raised its ugly head in a big way, and that was truly my first real direct encounter with the beast. My next step was to find out how I scored on the test, sue the Town of Selma, and continue my education. Well, reality set in, and I realized it was only me with my limited resources. It was me against city hall. I had no father or family member that could help me sustain such a fight, so I plotted my course for departure. Before I left, I asked the chief a couple of times to see my test results, but his first excuse was the town attorney had the test. Then, he told me the tests were all destroyed. Most of my peers would say I'm a fool for not slapping the town with a lawsuit, but they would have never understood from the outside looking in, and I wasn't about to take on a battle I didn't have a chance on winning. Sergeant McDonald and I discussed it, and he understood it, but he could do nothing to help as badly as he probably wanted to. Before I left Selma, I continued my education, graduated from college, and quickly applied with the North Carolina Alcohol Law Enforcement, a division of the Crime Control and Public Safety of North Carolina, which falls under the authority of the governor. I got the job and left Selma with hopes of never returning.

After going through eighteen months of rigorous physical and academic training, I became an alcohol law enforcement agent and was stationed in Fayetteville, North Carolina, the home of Fort Bragg, the largest military institute in the country. Working for ALE was a unique experience. Unique in that there was little supervision, a lot of freedom, but a lot of responsibility. I got a chance to make my own hours and to take full charge of any complaints as well as find resolutions for each. I was assigned two very large counties, Scotland and Robeson, and I knew I had my work cut out for me. I quickly formed a close bond with a couple of wonderful people who graduated from the academy with me. We shared a lot of laughs together and a lot of problems and issues within the agency. My friends and I remained close during my tenure with the agency where I remained for about two years until I became a bit overzealous in my efforts to be the best.

While I was out with other agents on special operation, I forgot to do an equipment maintenance check on an Alco-Sensor, an alcohol detection kit. I knew I would have to do a barrage of paperwork for performing a late test, so I decided to falsify the document by entering an incorrect time, which was beyond the deadline. That one incident caused my boss to question my credibility, sincerity, and integrity on the job. My boss and I agreed that I could no longer work under those conditions, so I resigned. Soon after, I contacted a man who offered me a job a year earlier while I was still employed with ALE. That man was Robin Mallory, the chief of police in Lawrence. Chief Mallory had always told me, if I ever wanted a job, to give him a call. Well, guess what, I needed a job. I called him, told him what I was going through, and he hired me just like that. I resigned from ALE and became a police officer for the City of Lawrence.

CHAPTER 3

My New Home

This would mark my first experience having an African American boss, and it was truly a unique experience meeting this man the natives knew as Robin for the first time in 1990. I was so conditioned throughout my career to speak in the usual official police tone that it caught me off guard when he and I met for the first time a year ago, and he introduced himself to me. It was almost like we were talking in the coffee shop. He extended his hand to me and said in a stern and heavy voice but pleasant smile, "I'm Robin Mallory, and your name again is...?" After our introduction, conversation came with ease, and he made me feel like I was already part of his regiment. As a matter of fact, it was during our first meeting that he offered me the job I eventually accepted. This was a man I quickly came to admire because he was the man I wanted to be. He was black like me, he spoke like me, he was respected, and he was the chief.

I could only imagine the opposition he faced during his early tenure in policing, but obviously, he stood the test of time. I quickly realized that Chief Mallory was not just a chief in a small town, but a friend to the people and a mentor to most. He was invited to almost all civic and social functions and eased right in to just about any affair. He seemed to really enjoy his work and being part of the community he called home. Another odd quality that made him different from most public officials I have met was the fact he loved to write poems. He finally published a book entitled, *A Book of Poems*, in

2003. He later started mass marketing his product and made a pretty penny doing so.

Whether it was by virtue of his position or by his character, most folks in Lawrence, especially in the African American community, wanted to somehow be connected to him in some way. He created poems for any occasion imaginable and would read them at the various functions when requested. He created poems on eloquent plaques for state and federal agencies, bereaving families, birthdays, anniversaries, weddings, and the list goes on. His lucrative business allowed his name to be stretched far from home, and it made him loved by many.

Chief Mallory's immediate family, including his wife who worked in a local factory and his two sons who graduated from the local high school, were all born and bred in this town, and there were very few people that any of them didn't know. When I used to accompany him on his quick trips to the store or to his home, we would often be stopped by one of his many admirers who just wanted to say hello. The ten-minute trip sometimes turned out to be an hour or two. He couldn't even stand in the department's parking lot for ten minutes unless he was disturbed by at least two people vying for his attention. I didn't think there was a soul in the town that disliked him. He could easily run for just about any political office in our county and probably win by a landslide. He had the charisma, the dark-complexioned look, the deep voice, and the stature of a Lawrence landmark. I still often think of Chief Mallory, and I truly thank him for bringing me to Lawrence and giving me a sense of normalcy and placement. Lawrence is not a metropolitan by any stretch of the imagination, but it was comfortable, and it was home.

Lawrence was a quaint and sleepy town back in the summer of 1991 when I started patrolling the streets. It was a southern town where the population was still just over 17,000 and filled with ordinary people. There was a mixture of working and nonworking class, but for the most part, people were decent and respectful, somewhat unlike modern times. It was a rare occasion that something big and newsworthy happened. Sure, ordinary things happened in the criminal world like petty thefts, burglaries, assaults, and sometimes even a homicide or two. But most crimes were solved relatively quickly because the town was a small, somewhat close-knit community where everybody knew everybody, and most of the residents that lived there were related in some form or fashion. Most of the police department were comprised of homegrown individuals who made it very easy to acquire information from their own friends and relatives. This was home for a lot of my counterparts, and again, I found myself as an outsider, but I managed to fit in quite well.

There was really nothing special about Lawrence other than being awarded the all-American city for several years in a row. I never knew the full extent of what being an all-American city meant, but I knew it had something to do with the enrichment of the community and the collaboration between the community and government to foster growth. Whatever it meant in the fullest extent was probably a good thing, and I guessed that it was something to be proud of.

Lawrence was no different than any other city and not as attractive as others. It's simply divided into four sectors of north, south, east, and west. The north side contained small mom-and-pop-type businesses, such as convenience stores and washerettes. It also contained only about two or three nice neighborhoods comprised of mostly African American. The south side contained more chain-operated businesses and more affluent neighborhoods. The east side consisted of low-income housing with a few businesses sporadically spread here and there among the neighborhood. The west side consisted of older neighborhoods that were once inhabited by the upper class of the area. But as time progressed, the houses got older, and the incomes got smaller. It was obvious to see the changing of the times.

Just like most other neighborhoods in the region, the neighborhoods in Lawrence began to go through a transition. A transition from a peaceful and serene place where parents allowed their children to play freely outside without a care in the world to one of violence and drugs. Every day, when I used to ride through the neighborhoods, I saw children playing, laughing, and just being kids in a world they knew and was accustomed to. I saw their parents and knew a lot of them by name and their smiling faces. Most of them would wave at me either because they knew me or just because I was "the law" as they called me. There was no better thrill than to see the calm of the streets as we used to call it. If a crime happened, it was usually committed by an acquaintance whose name would pop up from the onset of the investigation. So it really didn't take much of an investigation to bring those cases to an end. Lawrence was full of good people, people who didn't mind helping one another no matter what the case was. I admired that most about the place we called home. Everyone treated me really nice, and they always had a smile to offer, especially the shopkeepers and retailers. I especially enjoyed going to the local grocery store (Food Lion) where I often caught the eye of a young female manager. Every time I went into that store, I always found her with that pleasant smile that could have easily advertised a Colgate toothpaste commercial. She was the girl with the Colgate smile. It seemed she worked all the time but never looked tired, and when somebody needed help, she was Johnny-on-the-spot. It was clear she was a hard and dedicated employee, and I knew she had the makings of top-level management. As I continued to shop at this same neighborhood grocer, the young lady and I began to exchange a few words here and there. She was substantially younger than I, but she carried herself in an attractive, mature fashion. I would have recommended her to any decent young suitor. I never knew her name and never knew where she lived, but little did I know, there would eventually come a time when Arnita Hatcher and I would become closer than ever.

 I stayed in the patrol division for about two and a half years performing the menial tasks that quickly became of little interest to me. I busted my butt like everyone else and kept my nose clean because I had a desire to do something more and something different. Not that the patrolman's job was any less important than any other, but I felt I wanted to make more of a contribution and make more of a difference in people's lives. I wanted people to know I existed and appreciate the service I was capable of providing. I had an associate's degree in applied science from Johnston Community College and a bachelor's degree from North Carolina Central University. Writing parking tickets, investigating accidents, and walking the beat was not fulfilling for me, and it wasn't where I wanted to be. I did enjoy police work though, but I was serious minded about the job and focused on my career path. I often conveyed my feelings and desires to my supervisor as well as the chief since he was the ultimate decision maker on who gets promoted. Although I was a transplant from somewhere else, my supervisor quickly recognized my potential, initiative, and efficiency when dealing with investigative matters. After recognizing my somewhat of a skill level in investigations, he pushed for me to get more training in the field. Not only did he push for my training, he spoke to the chief on my behalf and recommended me for a detective's position if it ever became available.

After two years of hard time, the position I dreamed of became available after a senior detective retired. I'm sure I made a few heads swirl after making such a move in record time, but I never heard any adverse remarks. However, it doesn't mean that there were none. I felt in my heart that I was ready and qualified. I held two degrees, I conducted major investigations for ALE, I received specialized training in the field, and I was highly motivated and recommended by a veteran supervisor. Apparently, the chief thought I was qualified as well as he was the ultimate decision maker at the time, and he seemed to take an interest in me regarding the position.

One day, he unexpectedly called me into his office and had quite an interesting but short conversation with me about Jackson Poesley, the lieutenant of detectives. At first, he kept me waiting for just a few minutes in silence as he often did as he finished reading whatever he had in his hand. He finally looked at me with sort of a blank look and asked me if I really wanted the position and if I was serious about it. I quickly told him yes and wondered why he asked me such a ridiculous question. Another minute of cold silence went by, which caused me great concern because I didn't know what was coming next. That minute of waiting seemed like a lifetime. As I steadily gazed at him with perplexity, he continuously looked down on his desk. I couldn't tell what he was looking at, but I assumed it was my application. He finally looked up and asked me, "Are you sure you can handle Lieutenant Poesley?" It was at that point my muscles started to relax, the tension faded, and I regained my confidence all in about five seconds. "Yes, sir, I think so," I said. The chief went on to inform me that the lieutenant was "hell with a pen." He said he writes down everything, and he was a stickler for documentation, so I had better be right if I was going to be successful in the position. Being a serious-minded individual and dedicated to my profession, I repeated myself and told the chief again with confidence, "I think I can handle it." "All right," he said, "that's all I need to know." I then walked out of his office, knowing in the back of my mind and saying to myself that I was going to be the next detective. I was subsequently promoted to the rank of detective.

CHAPTER 4

Moving Forward

In the past two years of my employment with the police department, I cannot recall ever having any lengthy conversations with the lieutenant. As I think about it now, I don't think I've ever had a conversation with him at all. I do remember speaking to him in passing from time to time and him calling out my name as he reported for work in the mornings. His office was not in the main portion of the building where most of the officers congregated or exchanged information. His office was in a separate hallway that was always quiet. After he reported for work, he would not be seen or heard from again unless it was time for lunch or quitting time. So I really didn't know what his job function was until I became part of the division. The day before I was to report to him, he saw me in the lobby of the police department and said in a loud and somewhat-intimidating voice, "Monroe, be in my office at eight o'clock sharp, eight o'clock sharp, and we dress in suit and tie." He said it in front of everyone who was in earshot distance. He was quite loud and stern as if he really didn't want me to be part of the division. I could not tell one way or the other.

The lieutenant was a short dark-complexioned man and a little heavy around the waist, but he wore it well. He had short salt-and-pepper hair and was always well polished, adorned with his fine suits and shined Florsheim shoes. He walked with a fast pace as if he was always on a mission. Where the mission was, I never knew, but he always looked like he was on one. Even after his thunderous voice penetrated my body, I was on cloud nine, and I wasn't about to let anything or anyone shake me, including the lieutenant.

I reported to work the following day dressed in a suit and tie as requested and stood ready for anything tossed in my direction. The usual job of the new kid on the block was to take on everything that the senior detectives didn't want. Instead, I spent the day getting acclimated to the division. The lieutenant first assigned me my gear, which consisted of a Glock semiautomatic model .22 handgun, Remington rifle, ammunition, two-way radio, and tan Crown Victoria that was spotless. He assigned me an office and everything else that came along with the role of detective. I knew the division was much more than where I came from with the patrol. I immediately acquired things and responsibility I would have never acquired with patrol. My own car, office phone, cell phone, clothing allowance, freedom, a substantial raise, and an abundant amount of overtime were just some of the things I enjoyed about the position. After the lieutenant assigned my gear, he sat me down in his office and closed the door. It was at this time I knew he was a no-nonsense kind of guy. He told me in no uncertain terms what he expected of me, and he didn't need anyone he had to babysit. "So if you can't cut it, you don't need to be here!" He explained to me how the division was like a family and how he believed in professionalism, which is what the division was all about. *Professionalism.* He drilled that word in my head several times throughout our conversation, and he made sure I didn't forget it. He probably thought he was intimidating me or scaring me, but little did he know, I appreciated what I was being told because I believed in the same standards. The more he spoke, the more I admired the man we called lieutenant. He was serious-minded. He was well spoken. When he spoke, anyone would know he was clearly the head of the division, and he didn't mind people knowing it. This was what I asked for, where I wanted to be, and what I worked for. I knew by the end of our conversation, the lieutenant and I would get along just fine.

The division consisted of three other detectives: Audrey Woodland, Myer Kimmel, and the narcotics detective, Gene Murcey. It also consisted of a juvenile officer, Brendle McQuail, and a crime scene and evidence technician, Kent Stoney. I learned all I could from all my new partners, and they taught me well. After just a few weeks, they seem to let me take the lead in some of the cases. I didn't know if their actions were to set me up for failure or gear me toward success. Of course, as always, I was the only African American in a pool of white Caucasians, which sometimes clogged my head with negative thoughts based on my history back in Johnston County. I gladly took the lead though. I thought it was fun, invigorating, and fulfilling, and it seemed to be my niche.

Upon the fourth week, Audrey Woodland, the senior detective, told the lieutenant how well I was adapting, and he recommended I begin my solo career. The lieutenant seemed pleasantly surprised, looked at me with a smile, and agreed with Audrey's recommendation. I no longer had to shadow anyone or report to anyone other than the lieutenant. I still knew I could call on any of my partners in the division if I needed help as they all let me know they had my back. It was beginning to feel like a family atmosphere just as I was told.

We all grew pretty close as we ate breakfast together every morning before we started our office assignments. It was during breakfast that we got a chance to let our hair down and discuss whatever we wanted with no holds barred. Sometimes the conversation would be about personal issues, and at other times, it was all business. We learned a lot about each other and grew even closer as the years progressed. We've endured many ordeals between each other and discussed them all like marriages, divorces, children being born, houses being purchased, houses being sold, financial burdens and financial gains. It was like we were each other's spouses for eight hours a day and five days a week because we all knew each other's problems, and we worked sometimes collectively to solve them or help in some way. Sometimes just listening to each other was enough.

I remember one of the first homicides I was assigned. It was an interesting one, but we were able to close the case after arresting multiple people. I received a phone call from the police department about one o'clock in the morning, about a man found dead on the patio of an apartment. Charles Freeman was his name and apparently, he collapsed while sitting outside on the patio chair. Once we started investigating the death, we found several people who was involved with his death to include Robert Lovin, Tony Singletary, Jamaal McDonald, James Massey, and Donnell Massey. It was told by one of the suspects that, Charles was in possession of illegal drugs which he may or may not have sold to make money. The suspects cornered him in the back of the apartment complex where they beat him severely in search of drugs. Freeman fought for his life as he tried to get away from the suspects, but the over-powered him and continuously hit him with their fists, kicked him, hit him with metal trash cans, and even hit him with a bicycle. Nobody ever admitted to finding drugs on Freeman, but as he seemed to lay almost lifeless, they stopped beating him, and everybody scattered and left him for dead except one suspect, Robert Love. Robert got him up from the ground and literally carried him to a nearby patio chair where, Freeman collapsed and died. Robert left the scene without knowing Freeman died.

    The case was difficult to investigate because there were no witnesses at the time, and nobody wanted to get involved. One day, Charles' sister Lorraine came to my office and sat down where we began to talk. She told me about Charles and told me he was basically a good person, but she didn't condone what he did in his life, and she didn't have anything to do with him when it came to his choices. Lorraine seemed very sincere and remorseful for what occurred to her brother. She didn't seem angry in the least bit or seeking revenge. She only asked that her brother's killers be brought to justice. Lorraine told me she was a Christian and she believes in her relationship with the Lord. She went on to tell me the Lord let her know anyone, and all the people involved in her brother's murder would be brought to justice. She told me to continue my path and the information would be revealed to me. She said they all might not face justice at the same time, but every one of them will pay the price for what they did. I thanked her for talking about the matter and asked her to call me if she receives any information about the murder. That was the first and only time I saw Lorraine until almost two years later.

CHAPTER 5

Atmospheric Shift

All was going normal and well with the department and within the division until October of 1993 when Chief Mallory received a dreadful and tragic phone call from a representative of Shaw University, which was located in Raleigh, North Carolina. The call was about his firstborn son who was in his sophomore year at the university. He learned that his son died by his own hands after playing a game of Russian roulette while on campus. If I am not mistaken, I believe it was the chief who gave his son the handgun as a gift as we fathers sometimes do. Sometimes the man in us doesn't think about the possible repercussions that come from the decisions we make. Some repercussions are insurmountable, and this was truly one of those times. I could not imagine the pain and despair that came along with that phone call. He briefly told the lieutenant what happened as he left the office in a silent panic. There wasn't much talk about the tragedy in the chief's absence, but the word spread pretty quickly throughout the city. People would ask me about it, but I really couldn't tell them much other than what was told to me. So everyone continued to work as normal as we wondered what really happened. Did his son really kill himself, or did somebody kill him? It didn't seem quite right that such a nice young man would do something so stupid. Personally, I thought it was a homicide until we were all told differently by the chief after he returned to the job weeks later. His son did in fact kill himself while playing the game of Russian roulette.

After his return, the chief never allowed anyone to share his pain or give him consolation. For anybody that asked, he would tell them what happened as if he was talking about a routine investigation. It was like he never went through a grieving period; at least that I could see. I often asked him if he was okay, and he would cordially respond in his usual deep solemn voice as he looked away, "Yeah." Every now and then, he would have a few more words to say about the tragedy as if he was trying to find answers to something that seemed obvious. I guess the feeling of denial is part of the death process. I became rather close to the chief since being part of the division, and I got to know him and his actions quite well. My office was right next door to his. I knew his daily routine and behaviors, and I certainly knew his abnormalities. He reported for work each day with what he thought was his normal look, but it was nothing but a facade. He wanted people to know how poised and in control he was, but I could see right through and beyond what I think other people could not. I wanted to talk to him more, but I didn't know if he would be receptive to someone younger like me, but then again, who was I to question his emotions? In my mind, I felt that he would eventually get it out and deal with it just like everyone else. But somebody forgot to tell him that bereavement was a part of all our lives, and it's all right to lament in the loss of our loved ones.

The chief never quite recovered from that dreadful phone call, and I think a large piece of him was left where he laid his son to rest. He became somewhat despondent and distant, almost like he was in a world of his own. Current events of the city didn't seem to bother him anymore. As a matter of fact, nothing seemed to bother him at all. He was numb and carried himself in somewhat of a robotic fashion. A lot of us backed away because we didn't know how to handle it or what to say. The look on his face told us daily that he didn't want to be bothered. The man I knew and admired never came back to us the way he left. I thought he would soon retire after that ordeal, but he remained and tried his best to return to the chief we all knew. Everyone simply settled for who he had become. Besides, we didn't have much of a choice.

I continued my career as a detective and excelled as time progressed. I often received compliments from my counterparts for my work as well as annual merit raises. The other detectives would often ask me to accompany them during their investigations because I seemed to connect with people in an effortless sort of way. I usually solicited confessions on most of my cases, which was the ultimate thrill for me and the nail in the coffin for others. Being in the detective investigative worked great for me. Take out my clothes were paid for and I wore nice clothes, I got a chance to really help people who couldn't otherwise help themselves, and I was able to meet a whole new circle of people I most likely would have never connected with if not for the division.

CHAPTER 6

Moonlighting

Some of the interesting people within the circle were the owners, operators, and general manager of one of our local motels; the Ramada Inn, which housed a nightclub named Capers. I first became familiar with the folks at Capers through a case of missing money, otherwise known as the crime of embezzlement. It was owned by a private corporation and managed by a guy named Ron Boyer. The case was successfully closed, but during the investigation, I developed relationships and good rapport with most staff members. The manager noticed my work ethics and eventually told me he liked the way I was able to connect with people. He asked me to make an appearance in the club every now and then to make it appear to his patrons that there was police presence around the establishment. It actually gave them a sense of false security, but if it helped, I was not opposed to the idea. Periodically, a fight or two would break out during the weekend, and I guess my presence was Ron's way of curtailing those unwanted activities. Ron told me he really couldn't pay me for doing it, but he could get me discounts on hotel rooms when I traveled. I saw nothing wrong with what he asked of me, and I took him up on the offer.

I would stop in about three or four times a week, speak to some of the patrons, and leave. Most people would think getting discounted rooms was not an adequate form of compensation in contrast to what I should have been paid. But I did travel a lot, and the discounted room rates really came in handy. I continued to perform my menial service until the establishment incurred financial problems beyond repair, and the company filed for bankruptcy. I assumed it was the beginning of my end with the establishment, but Ron allowed me to continue doing what I did best for him, which was deter troublemakers from making trouble. I enjoyed doing it because it gave me an opportunity to talk with the people of Lawrence in a relaxed and social setting when they were free to say exactly what was on their minds. Although most of them would have consumed a beer or two or six, mostly everyone respected me as a police officer. They were able to state their innermost thoughts about their personal problems. Some patrons complained about the city government, others complained about the mayor and about the chief as well as officers on the force whom they liked or didn't like for one reason or another.

CHAPTER 7

The Hatchers

As I continued to perform my duties at the Ramada Inn, I saw quite a few employees come and go. Some were good employees, and some should have been fired way before their departure. I was fortunate though to meet one of the good employees by the name of Sallie Hatcher. She was the older sister of Arnita, the girl in the grocery store with the Colgate smile. Not only was Arnita attractive and shapely, but Sallie was equally appealing and robust with a body that any man could admire. She was different than her sister Arnita in that she was very outspoken and said whatever she was thinking and didn't care who liked it or who didn't. She was the type that could intimidate any introverted guy because she had a certain level of confidence about her. However, I wasn't sure if that level of confidence was because she was genuinely confident of herself or because it was her way of shielding her shortcomings from the world. Either way, she appeared to be a happy and jovial person who was usually in a good mood on any given work night. She was a single mother of two children. One child, Gabrella, was by her Puerto Rican boyfriend Ricardo Delsado. Ricardo was a handsome fellow who aspired to make something of himself in a world that was full of closed doors. He was a student at Pembroke State University in Pembroke, North Carolina, where he joined the fraternity of Alpha Psi Alpha. Her other child, Isaac, was the son of a forgotten relationship. Isaac's father was completely out of the picture and never volunteered any support for his son, and Sallie never pursued any. Ricardo had been the closest man in Sallie's life that had influence and brought some meaning to her otherwise-reckless life.

It was rumored in the streets and among club goers that Sallie was a good-time girl. Even though she was part of the have-nots, she loved to have fun, and she could effectively communicate with anyone. Her ability to connect with people, especially the customers, was a unique characteristic she mastered. It was said she dated several men, but of course, nobody ever really had any concrete information about the rumors. To me, she seemed like a normal young lady who did no more than any other single lady of her age. She was pretty and bold without any shyness about her, which was easy to tell as she bounced around the nightclub performing her waitressing tasks. She was easy to look at, and the men didn't mind letting her know it. They often teased her about her shapely posterior and bodacious breasts, but she just returned the tease and kept working. Sallie was a good waitress, and she knew how to work the crowd. Just when some of the guys thought they might partner up with her for the night or in the near future, she made a quick exit when her shift was over and left them drooling and wondering as men do after being disappointed. She always left alone, and sometimes, I would even walk with her to her car to make sure she left safely. I didn't know a lot about her, but I often wondered what else she did for a living besides waitressing. She was very articulate, assertive, and smart, and she walked like no other waitress. She walked in a commanding yet sexy manner with her back and shoulders arched as if she had some level of formal instruction.

She eventually quit working the club scene and literally dropped out of sight for quite some time. I didn't know why she quit, but I found out shortly thereafter that she wanted to pursue her career in teaching. I heard from some reliable sources that she was pulling her life together and ridding herself of all the negative shadows that plagued her life. Shedding the waitress suit and people's perception of her was her primary goal. She finished her education and became a certified teacher at Washington Park Primary School. I never saw her again, but I heard she was doing well and was liked by students and teachers alike. I thought it was great that she would better herself by pursuing her career in teaching. I'm sure it was tough growing up on the north side of town and breaking the molehill of poverty that surrounded her for most of her life.

The Hatcher family resided in an old, dingy white wooden house on the corner of North Main Street and Alder Road. It was encased by other houses of like structure and section 8 apartments. The wood of the house looked like it had never been painted and appeared almost like the color of aged putty. One dropped match could have brought an end to this loving dwelling place where most of the family lived. The house was dark and very dreary inside with little decor if any. As I often looked at the house during my routine business, I had to wonder why they were living in those conditions. There was LeRue, a well-abled mechanic father who lived in the house along with Adele, his well-abled wife. Arnita and Sallie also lived in the house and obviously were contributing financially because they both worked. Even though the conditions were substandard in a lot of folks' eyes, there was one thing that would take me away from any negative thoughts of their home, and that was the happiness I felt when I saw either of them. Jamaya was the oldest of the siblings, Sallie was next, then Arnita, and then came the youngest of the Hatcher sisters, Terri. The whole family seemed very nice, obviously intelligent and fun loving.

I would usually see their dad outside in the afternoons underneath the hood of somebody's car. He would be darkened not only by his complexion, but by the oil and soot from vehicles he had crawled under for that day. He too seemed to be a pleasant man based on the times I passed by his house and spoke in conversation or saw him outside. He seemed to be a somewhat-quiet man who talked but didn't really get involved in matters that didn't concern him. He seemed to be just one of the good ole homeboys the neighborhood knew and trusted with their cars whenever trouble struck. He apparently was a pretty good mechanic because it seemed like everyone in the neighborhood brought their cars to him to fix. I'm sure LeRue didn't have a formal education, but somehow, he eventually landed a job at Walmart in the automotive section where he continued his trade. Neither of the Hatcher family really knew me, but I was aware of them and grew with them as time passed. Little did I know I would become privy to some of the family's deepest and most intimate secrets.

Success doesn't come easy, and it does not come without consequences. It takes endurance, resilience, and perseverance to deal with and overcome the consequences. Jamaya, Sallie, Arnita, and Terri had to deal with those consequences throughout their younger years. In the early years, when the sisters were still innocent and naive about the world and all the evil things that plagued it, they encountered devastation that no child should have to endure, but many do. That devastation was molestation by their father. Nobody dared to discuss it inside or outside the home, and it remained a family secret until it was revealed to me. I certainly understood why it was a well-kept secret. It would have torn the family apart mentally as well as physically and possibly wind the siblings in foster care or be left without their father, the provider.

Since being involved in investigations and learning more about social issues, it became apparent that many households had encountered molestation and incest. It's often kept within the family or within oneself for fear of repercussions from the antagonist, being ridiculed or ostracized by society, or even being emotionally detached from the family. The more I learned about LeRue, the more I realized he was no different than the rest of the no-good, deadbeat dads in the world, and he was no longer the man I thought I knew. I guess the adage holds true: you can't judge a book by its cover. Not only did the girls give their parents respect, but they respected the family as a whole and would not do anything to go against the moral turpitude of their family sanctities, no matter what, until they were old enough to think independently. Once the sisters became old enough to realize the father they respected in their adolescent years was a deadbeat, womanizing, child molester, they became more vocal with both LeRue and their mother. But never did they discuss their family affairs outside the home. Terri, the youngest of the girls, was too young to know or understand what was going on. She managed to escape the drama after she graduated from high school and moved away to attend college. Like a lot of mothers, Adele was aware but was not very vocal on the subject matter. She loved her family dearly, and I'm sure she was in somewhat of the same position facing her daughters.

CHAPTER 8

The Takeover

Like Sallie, I eventually decided to take a break from the Ramada Inn because of internal issues regarding bankruptcy, an action that was almost inevitable. Owners and managers started betraying one another, taking money, underordering merchandise to save money, and doing underhanded business deals. They looked for me to investigate several matters since I was part of the establishment, but I decided to bail out to avoid getting in the middle of in-house squabbles. I was a lot wiser than I looked, and I wasn't about to get caught up in something that would reflect negatively with my real job at the police department. Things got even worse for the establishment, and they finally had to put the business up for sale.

Months later, a deal was brokered for well over a million dollars between the owners of the Ramada and a multimillion-dollar business tycoon out of New York City whom none of us had ever met. It took several weeks for the deal to be packaged and ready for sale, but the day finally came when the deal was agreed upon. The deal was brokered by the partners of the business tycoon, but the tycoon himself had never stepped foot in the establishment until the day of closing. That was the day Clyburn Gray came to Lawrence to seal the deal and take over the motel.

What happened next really didn't surprise me, but it did for a lot of other people. The owners of the establishment knew the buyer's name to be Clyburn Gray, but never did they realize that Mr. Clyburn Gray was a black man, and neither did I! The day he made his appearance to purchase the property was the day the owners declined to sell and completely removed it from the bargaining table. The racist owners would rather go bankrupt than sell their property to a black man.

The year was 2001, and racism was still in existence, contrary to what a lot of people thought or wanted to believe. The owners did everything they could to keep the business running but fell far short of accomplishing their goal. A year or so later, the business went into foreclosure and once again became part of the bargaining table. The savvy business tycoon got the word on the foreclosure, traveled to Lawrence again, and subsequently purchased it from the front steps of the Scotland County courthouse. He then became the new owner of what would later be known as the Clyburn Inn.

Mr. Gray didn't frequent Lawrence much, and I surely understood why. Coming from a place he came from, Lawrence was probably a lost colony, which made me wonder why a man of his stature wanted to live in such a desolate place. I guess a man of his wealth either needed a tax write-off or wanted a front for some illegal money-laundering operations. Little did I know I was far from the truth. I eventually met the man and quickly grew a level of respect for him after I was able to talk to him and understand his existence. Mr. Gray became an integral part of the Hatcher house as he still is today. As the chapters continue, they will reveal the full history of the man known as Gray.

CHAPTER 9

The Discovery

As I continued learning and progressing within the police department, I took on other responsibilities as well. One of those responsibilities was to learn the craft of crime-scene investigations, which most people of today refer to as CSI. I worked endless hours performing not only my tasks, but the tasks of the CSI, because the person in place during that time was scheduled to retire in the upcoming months. I suppose I was knighted and overburdened with this responsibility either because I was a fast learner, or the chief just didn't want to pay anybody else to do it. I was already a part of the division and knew all the internal workings, so it was an easy transition for me when it was necessary. I got a chance to go different places and take classes that really enhanced my career and pretty much made me a valuable commodity. Even though there were sometimes relentless hours, and I could barely keep my eyes open during the day, it was worth every bit of it.

On Sunday, April 8, 2001, I went to Wilson, North Carolina, to attend a forensic photography class on behalf of the police department. I was to be there for the next three days, and I was sent there to learn the mechanics and forensic operation of a 35-millimeter camera and prepare those pictures for court observation. It was a quick getaway from work, which I took often just to get away from all the madness that came with the job. Most of the classes I attended didn't require too much of my time outside the classroom, and I thought this one would be no different. However, it was a little more intense than expected, and it did require some nighttime activity for obvious reasons. The Sunday before class was always a day of leisure. I found some good restaurants, some good television shows, and got a chance to catch up on some reading material I had brought with me. I figured this getaway would be no different than any other. By 11:00 PM, I was in my room and in the bed in preparation for Monday's class.

Monday started as a good day; we were introduced to the camera, its functions, such as shutter speed, light vs. artificial-light sensitivity, painting with light, flashbacks, etc. I learned a lot of terms only camera geeks knew the meaning of, but I found it quite interesting. I grew a new appreciation for the 35-millimeter camera and its capabilities. It was definitely a necessity for a CSI. Good photography should tell a story from beginning to end if operated by a qualified person. The photos should place the observer right in the middle of the crime and allow the observer to easily follow and understand what took place.

Monday was a typical day of training, but Tuesday was something totally different, and I remember it like it was yesterday. It was in the morning session of class that I was interrupted by the training coordinator who told me to step out of class to take a phone call. I didn't think it was anything of importance, but I knew it was the police department. It was nothing unusual for them to call me for various reasons since I had added responsibilities. The next dialogue between me and somebody at the police department catapulted me into another world where I never truly was able to get back into the swing of things within the classroom. I believe I was talking to Lieutenant Edwards, who eventually rose to be Lawrence's police chief. However, my memory and recollection somehow escaped me after I heard the words "Sallie Hatcher…she's been stabbed multiple times. Man, we got a mess!" I remember answering the questions on the phone the best I could concerning the whereabouts of different supplies he needed. But all I could think about was getting back home to be a part of the case.

My body went sort of numb because of my casual relationship with Sallie. I knew her; I talked with her often as we worked together at the club. This was the girl I walked to her car to keep her safe, this was the girl who didn't bother a soul and always kept to herself. I didn't believe what I was hearing. How could this be? What kind of animal could kill a pretty, vibrant young woman in this manner?

Investigations came easy for me, and I wasn't easily moved by most. It was like I was immune to emotions when working on cases, and I usually got the job done. Sallie Hatcher's death was not the usual for me, and it was somewhat personal. I was determined that the son of a bitch who did this would be found by me and would go down hard by me. I became angry, irritated, and impatient. I called Lieutenant Poesley on a couple of occasions before class was over and after class to ask him if I could return home and join the investigation. He simply refused and told me to stay put. He told me they had things covered, and everything would be taken care of. Our conversation put me a little more at ease about the situation because it sounded like the case would be quickly solved. The lieutenant didn't seem overly concerned as he spoke on the phone, but maybe I was overreacting because it was Sallie's death. Homicides in our small town were usually solved relatively quickly because of the small network population and community response. I couldn't wait to return home to get a firsthand look at how things transpired. I was bound and determined to find Sallie's killer if he wasn't found by the time I returned home.

I spoke with Detective Clyde Sardoms quite a bit by phone. He had been with the division for about two years and was a pretty good detective himself. I spoke with him several times throughout the day, and he gave me a detailed account of what happened and his hypothesis on how the murder was committed. Clyde was usually thorough and meticulous in his work, and I was proud to work with him on just about any case that came our way. But on this particular case, something was very wrong. As I spoke to Clyde several times by phone, I could hear the dissatisfaction within his voice. He had the sound of frustration, exhaustion, and a sort of aggravation. Anybody that knew Clyde knew he was a nice guy who tried his best to please people and not make waves. He wanted to be liked, but as the job of a detective, it was quite difficult to achieve that level of standard consistently. Clyde was sort of solemn in a way when he spoke to me, but I could tell there was a lot more to this case than he was revealing. He began to describe the case to me in detail.

Sallie Hatcher had moved out of her parents' home when she was old enough and wise enough to sustain on her own. She was twenty-three years young when she died. She lived at 1301-C Tara Drive, a subsidized apartment building that contained four other apartment dwellings consisting of apartments A through D of which were located beside one another. The apartments were so close to each other that voices could be heard from one neighbor to the next. All of Sallie's neighbors knew each other, and even though none of them really mingled with each other, they were there for each other. But what happened this time? Why didn't the neighbors hear Sallie's plea for help?

CHAPTER 10

The Homicide

Sallie's apartment was the typical two-bedroom apartment, which was neatly kept. The front door opened up into the living room. Straight ahead of the living room was a bar that separated it from the kitchen. Inside the kitchen was the rear sliding glass door that led to a small square cement cubicle patio encompassed by a wooden fence with a locking mechanism. Between the living room and the kitchen is a hallway on the right that led to the bathroom, two bedrooms, hall closet, and attic. As you walk down the hall, Sallie's bedroom was at the rear on the right. Her children Gabrella and Isaac's room was to the left and just a few feet away from their mother's room. Tan carpet covered most of the floors with the exception of the kitchen and the bathroom, which was covered by linoleum.

Ordinarily, it was very orderly and quiet in the neighborhood until a fifteen-year-old female called 911 on that dreadful day. She told the dispatcher that a lady had been stabbed and to send the police. The caller's voice was elevated as she spoke frantically with the dispatcher. When officers arrived, a crowd was already beginning to form as the fifteen-year-old girl directed the police to apartment 1301-C, the home of Sallie Hatcher. What the officers saw next was something that hardly any of them had ever seen before.

Clyde described the scene as "just awful." The front part of the apartment was unblemished to a degree as was the hallway that led to the bedrooms. The bathroom and children's room were also normal, but when the officers entered Sallie's bedroom, it became nothing less than a horror story. Blood was strewn everywhere throughout the room as if it were a slaughterhouse. There was blood all over the floor, on the walls, and on the ceiling. The way Clyde described what he saw was unimaginable. As he continued his description, I became angrier at myself for not being there. I became angry with Lieutenant Poesley because he wouldn't let me return, and I was angry at a killer I didn't even know for slaughtering a girl I did know. I've investigated multiple homicides, but this one undoubtedly sounded like the worst.

It was like her killer enjoyed taking her life or just couldn't stop stabbing her once he started. The many drops of blood on the floor near her bed that I later observed was most likely where he began the massacre as she lay asleep in what she thought was her safe and secure refuge for her and her small children. The knife penetrated so deep and so many times into Sallie's body that blood continuously dripped from the blade. Not only did blood drip from the blade, it also dripped and flowed from Sallie's body as she became lifeless. The blood on the walls near her bed were signs of struggle as she tried to stay alive, but was overpowered, killed, and raped by this unknown monster. It was unclear if she was raped before or after death.

The blood on the ceiling was consistent with someone raising a knife overhead full of blood and then going full throttle forward, striking his/her victim. The sharp streaks and angles of blood on the ceiling defined the force, consistency, and momentum used by her assailant to stab her repeatedly about the upper body, her back, and even in her head. She was stabbed a total of twenty-five times according to the autopsy. It was obvious Sallie Hatcher struggled, but once she became incapacitated, there was no more hope to defend herself or her helpless children who were also in the apartment. She was helpless and at the total mercy of a man that cared nothing about her, a man who was purposely there to kill her and rape her. It was a miracle the children survived this massacre.

The lieutenant found several items of evidence in the bedroom to include dark-brown electrical cord, a dingy white shoestring, and what appeared to be a pepper-like substance lightly sprinkled on the floor. The room itself was like something one would only see on television. Two officers on the scene did not have the stomach to observe for very long. They both became queasy and went outside to regurgitate as they gasped for air. It was truly a scene that would have given anyone nightmares according to Clyde.

But the disheveled room was nothing compared to what the killer did to Sallie. Her naked body lay lifeless as it was positioned face up across her bed with only her blood-drenched bra still attached to her body. Even though her bra was still fastened, one side of it exposed her breast as if it had been pulled down for some erotic pleasure. Blood covered most of her body from the back to the front, but the stains seemed to concentrate around her head and face area as I later got my first observation from photographs. Her legs were stretched apart, and her ankles and wrist were bruised with ligature marks as if she had been tied up, but we had only found one shoestring. She was stabbed so many times that it was impossible to count the stab wounds without an autopsy by the medical examiner. Not only was she stabbed, but she was beaten severely about the head with an unknown object that we never located. It was clear to me that Sallie had no chance to defend herself against her determined and insane attacker, and she had no chance at life as her killer mauled and molested her.

The lieutenant collected all the evidence he could find, but it wasn't nearly enough as I found out later when I returned to work. The lieutenant did the best job he could possibly do under the circumstances. He had no formal training in crime-scene investigations and pretty much winged his way through the scene without any direction or guidance. He did what he thought was the obvious, but to a trained investigator, there were mountains of evidence left behind untouched and unseen. I don't think I could have done too much better if I was present, but I would have had the sense to accept that fact and ask for help.

The North Carolina State Bureau of Investigation was always at our disposal, and we had a great rapport with them. The bureau could have and should have taken over the crime scene because of our lack of resources and experience. All it would have taken was a phone call, but nobody ever made that call. The bureau had agents specifically trained for homicide investigations, and they had specialized equipment and resources at their fingertips. Information they could obtain within an hour would probably take us two days to a week to obtain. The bureau had partnerships across the country with both state and federal agencies and could reach out to any of them in an instant. This crime was huge, too huge for us, and we desperately needed help.

The police department's focus was lost that day, and Sallie's importance diminished in a wave of egos and personalities. The Lawrence Police Department, specifically Lieutenant Poesley, did not favor asking for help from any agency for fear of looking substandard and inadequate. We were a good department, but we were a small department with very limited resources. As a matter of fact, if anyone would even speak of requesting assistance from the SBI, a scoff or chuckle by my counterparts would follow. It was clear to me during Sallie's death that the LPD would rather sacrifice an innocent life rather than put egos aside and investigate the case properly.

As I was told about the crime scene, I began to feel sorrow for not only Sallie, but for her family who put trust in us to do the right things. The general public is hardly ever aware of what police really do behind the scenes. From the outside looking in, it looked like all was well, and we were doing a fine job. But if they only knew the extent of our work or lack thereof, I'm sure it would have been a total shock. Sometimes, it even shocked me. It became easy to fall in the category of complacency because we were used to solving crime and solving them quickly, but as I wrote earlier, times and people were changing, but we were not changing with them.

CHAPTER 11

The Investigation Begins

On Thursday morning, I returned to work, and the conversations I had with my counterparts were astonishing. I became numb and angry all over again. It was a total disappointment to me that I was not a part of the initial bludgeoned death investigation that my associates had to endure. I was saddened by the brutal death of a young black female. I was saddened by hearing about her own child who had to witness the death of his mother. I became angry after hearing what took place at the crime scene, and I became bitter upon hearing who controlled the tempo of the investigation and what was done.

Lawrence was not ready for a crime of this unusual nature, but we readied ourselves with what resources we had and plunged in with both feet. I was told that Lieutenant Edwards and Sergeant Doug Isley were assigned to the crime scene, which is one of the most crucial and intricate parts of an investigation. The police department had little supplies to accommodate a crime of this magnitude, and it was literally embarrassing to those who knew better like the other detectives on hand. Lawrence PD didn't even have the smallest of supplies on hand. So the blame really can't be placed on the so-called crime-scene investigators but on the administration for allowing such a fiasco to unfold.

Our police department lacked the simplest items of necessity such as booties. I'm sure most readers are aware of what booties are and what an important role they play in the preservation of a crime scene. For those of you who do not know the significance, booties are canvas covers that fit over shoes to prevent contamination of evidence or the destruction of it. They allow investigators to walk freely about a designated area without leaving foreign particles behind. Most people are familiar as they are worn by doctors and other hospital staff in sterile environments. The Lawrence PD didn't have any booties at the time, so Edwards and Isley used makeshift booties made of plastic grocery bags they found somewhere. I don't know how they attached the bags to their ankles to prevent them from coming off or tearing, and I dare not to ask them such a question. But they do deserve praise for thinking of the necessity. Countless photos were taken inside and out of the apartment as well as of Sallie's body as it lay lifeless across the bed.

Neither the lieutenant nor the sergeant had any formal training in crime-scene investigation or forensic photography, and probably only 50 percent of the pictures were adequate. The rest were blurred; some were covered with a pink shadow, and others did not develop at all. They collected several items of evidence like clothing, underwear, and other telltale signs that nobody could identify because none of the items were labeled or documented properly. There was no way to tell how or where the items were seized. Therefore, the items taken were practically useless in the court of law.

They collected phone bills, which indicated recent phone calls to her boyfriend and others in the late night. Also found and collected was an insurance policy in the amount of fifty thousand dollars that was recently taken out by her boyfriend Ricardo Delsado, whom she had been dating on and off and who was also baby Gabrella's father. As I was told, Sallie's hands and feet were bagged by Edwards and Isley to preserve any suspect DNA evidence that may have been found. Bags that are placed over the victim's feet and hands are normally tied to the wrists and ankles to prevent DNA evidence, such as hair, fibers, blood, saliva, and any other foreign matter from escaping. Sallie Hatcher's pocketbook and cell phone were not located. Both the lieutenant and the sergeant were hard workers and dedicated to the profession, but they should have never been allowed to lead a crime-scene investigation. As the story continued, I was sure the scene was completely obliterated. Sallie's body was eventually taken from the home and sent to Chapel Hill for an autopsy to be performed.

Not only was I surprised at how the crime-scene investigation went, I was also floored at the half-ass investigation done by my counterpart Clyde Sardoms. His lackadaisical investigation was the ultimate devastation for me. Clyde was the lead investigator, and his work was much better than what he was telling me. This was not an example of his normal work; it was not him. He cared about people and took pride in getting his work right, but this time, something went terribly wrong. As Clyde continued to speak, I could sense he was not himself, and he too was frustrated about how the investigation went. He had no confidence in the investigation whatsoever, and he finally began to explain to me how it went down.

He told me he attacked the homicide just as we always did, but this one quickly went in a different direction, starting with the crime-scene investigation. He said when he got to the crime scene, he found several people inside the apartment. Bystanders, relatives, and other onlookers should always be forbidden into a crime scene for obvious reasons, but not on this occasion. The police had arrived on the scene, but they too stood around and allowed any and everybody who wanted to enter the house walk right in. Entrants should be on a need-to-know basis only, and only limited people needed to know. Normally, only a few people would be allowed inside consisting of minimal law enforcement personnel, emergency services, medical examiner, and maybe a close family member who could positively identify the decedent. Clyde said he couldn't even remember how many people he saw going in and out that day. The persons that shocked him the most was his own bosses, Lieutenant Poesley and Chief Mallory, who he found sitting on the living room sofa. They were talking with the unidentified people in the house and among themselves. What Clyde described to me was a nightmare, and he didn't know how to handle it. What was he to do? Tell his boss and supervisor to leave the scene? Yes, that's exactly what he should have done, but I knew Clyde's weakness was to get along with everyone and not make waves, so he let them remain until they decided to exit.

He had only been at the scene for a couple of hours when Lieutenant Poesley hurried everyone and told them to "wrap it up" so they could get out of there. Clyde couldn't believe what he was hearing, but the lieutenant was serious about evacuating the premises without any regard for the investigation or how much more had to be done. A crime scene of this particular magnitude would normally take anywhere from twelve to twenty-four hours depending on what had to be done. The investigators evacuated the premises in less than three!

Clyde continued telling me about the case, but somehow, his words became a murmur as my mind began to swirl in different directions. A good investigator is always thinking of ways to solve a problem. Even while people are talking, a detective is usually dissecting the information, organizing his/her thoughts, formulating opinions, and deciding how best to implement all those thoughts. I heard every word Clyde told me that day I returned to work, but I began analyzing only bits and pieces in order to figure out where we should restart the investigation.

What I did hear was that he and Detective Woodland questioned Ricardo Delsado, the baby's father, as well as Sallie Hatcher's estranged lover. Delsado showed up at the crime scene only moments after the police arrived. The obvious questions quickly came to mind. How did he get there? How did he get there so fast? Why was he there? How did he know, and where was he at the time of the murder? Clyde told me they talked with him briefly at the scene but soon after let him go. He told me they also questioned Jaston Setler who was allegedly another lover that frequented Sallie's apartment. Jaston had been seen with Sallie earlier on the same day she died. They also allowed him to leave after he briefly gave them an account of his whereabouts.

This was when the wrinkles started formulating on my forehead and my teeth started clinching together. I immediately ranked both Ricardo and Jaston as prime suspects in this case. From what I understood, Sallie was doing quite well and didn't date much at all, and Ricardo and Jaston were her two closest relationships. So why in the world wasn't Ricardo and Jaston drilled and interrogated properly? Why wasn't DNA evidence collected from them? Why didn't two seasoned detectives get a full statement from either two men? I didn't even care to think about or rationalize the whys and the whynots, but I knew these things had to be done. I'm sure Clyde knew me well enough to tell my mind was racing, and I truly believe that was why he shared the entire story of the homicide with me. I kind of had a way of getting things done in a pushy, arrogant sort of way, and I didn't really care whose toes I stepped on to get what I needed. Some people disliked me for my work ethics, and others appreciated it, especially the victims whom we were sworn to protect. At the end of the day, the victims are the only people that really matter to me. Most people cannot protect themselves, and most don't know how to protect themselves. We were paid and trained well to make sure they got that protection.

CHAPTER 12

More Work to Be Done

Clyde and I both knew that more had to be done to bring this case to a close, and we began to do what we always did. We exchanged information and came up with a list of things to do next. First and foremost, we had to go back to Sallie's apartment and collect any and all evidence that wasn't collected on the day of her murder. The apartment was relinquished to Sallie's family after the police finished the investigation. They began cleaning the apartment and salvaging anything that they needed or that reminded them of Sallie. As much as we hated to return to the apartment and face Sallie's family all over again, we had to do it for our own sake as well as theirs. The family graciously invited us in and gave us full consent to search and collect anything we deemed pertinent to the investigation. We looked and felt a little awkward returning to the home after several days had passed to search for evidence. Cleanup had taken place, items were misplaced and out of place. Evidence was surely contaminated or destroyed, but we knew that going in. We had to keep in mind that it was necessary if we were going to close this case.

Once Clyde and I were in the house, he walked me through the entire apartment as he told me his theories on how the murder may have happened. We walked in the front door, which opened into the living room. In that room, I saw a computer that had not been dismantled and left by my counterparts. Computers are a very good source of information, and the stuff that can be learned from someone's computer can be astronomical. It could have possibly been the vessel to solve Sallie's murder if someone dared to search the data inside. We seized the computer and had it transported to a forensic science lab for extraction. There was also a plethora of documentation, photos, letters, etc., scattered about the wooden entertainment center that housed her thirty-two-inch color television. I found letters she had wrote to Ricardo, which spoke about their relationship. A couple of the letters talked about her exhaustion with the relationship and how she wanted to move on in life without him. She talked about how the two of them were on two different paths in life. Sallie wanted to settle down and make a life and home for their baby girl Gabrella, but apparently, from her letters, Ricardo was not ready for that.

In a photo album, she had laid out the life she wanted with Ricardo in chronological order. The album started with pictures of her and Ricardo, then just her, then Ricardo and the baby. Another chapter seemed to begin when she posted pictures of herself trying on a wedding dress and her posing in a defined stance as she stood proud wearing her wedding gown. A pretty gown it was, and it looked quite expensive. The sequence of the photo album became very significant. She and Ricardo were so happy at one point in their lives that she was preparing herself for marriage, but something happened. But what? That was something Clyde and I had to figure out. There were lots and lots of pictures of Ricardo, as well as animated drawings and writings by Sallie that displayed the love she had for him. Whatever caused their demise had to be serious and had to be figured out. As playful and insignificant as the items looked to onlookers, they were important to us as detectives. We seized the items with hopes of using them against Ricardo when it came his turn to face a courtroom jury.

After looking and collecting evidence from the living room, we walked straight ahead into the kitchen and out of the back door where a wooden gate surrounded the patio. The cheaply manufactured locking mechanism had been broken, and it appeared to have been broken from the outside in. We couldn't tell if it was a fresh break or an old one that had not been repaired. Lieutenant Edwards had already collected the lock that was found on the ground on the patio. We looked for more evidence or any signs of an intruder but found nothing else. When I walked back in, I immediately scanned the kitchen and saw a single knife missing from the cutlery set, which sat atop of the sink's countertop. The cutlery set didn't appear to be disturbed in any way, and it was sitting next to other normal kitchen items like the toaster and bread box. It looked like Sallie probably removed the knife herself to do some slicing. Only one thing was out of the ordinary about the knife, and that was the fact that we did not find it. We looked everywhere. We thought it could be within the kitchen and other places, but we never found it. Maybe it was broken and tossed away, but either way, I wanted an explanation. We seized the cutlery set also.

As we walked out of the kitchen, we turned left to walk down a hallway that led to the bathroom on the left and two bedrooms. One of the bedrooms was where the children slept and felt the secure feeling of their mother lying right next to them in the adjacent bedroom. The house was fairly neat as we walked slowly down the hall. I kept wondering how this person got into this young lady's house. The front door wasn't damaged, the back sliding door wasn't damaged, and the cover for the attic didn't appear to be disturbed, although we didn't rule it out. The venting systems between the four apartments were connected. Therefore, it wouldn't be impossible for an individual to climb in the ceiling from one apartment to another. It would be a bit extreme, but criminals and delinquents have no boundaries when they are focused on what they want. The windows of Sallie's apartment were all intact. *It had to be an acquaintance*, I thought to myself as I walked. The walls were paper thin, and surely if someone forcefully and physically broke into the apartment, the neighbors would have heard something. I came to a conclusion even before I finished searching the apartment that she knew her killer. She welcomed him in; they talked for a while as he calculated how he was going to kill. He probably followed behind her as she walked into her bedroom for some reason. That was his opportunity to overtake her and have his way. Once he began his tyranny, he couldn't stop, and he wouldn't stop until Sallie was lifeless. In his mind, he could have her no other way than dead. Otherwise, she would have nothing to do with him, and he had nothing he could do for her. That was my first theory. Another theory was the locking mechanism was broken by the killer, and maybe somehow, he was able to get in the sliding door. It was difficult to validate any theory because of our absence at the crime scene.

What did Sallie do to deserve such barbaric treatment? Who did she piss off bad enough to kill her and mutilate her body in such a way to humiliate her? Only she had the answers to that, and she took them with her to the grave that day. But as we continued through the house, went into her bedroom, and collected several more items of evidence, I paused to ask the only person I knew that could help lead me in the right direction. That person was Sallie herself. I said a quick silent prayer and asked God to be with us on our journey to the truth. I asked Sallie to talk to me as I prayed and reveal to me who took her life. Crime scenes and bodies have a way of telling a story, and this was no different.

After collecting and temporarily storing the evidence, Clyde and I went over the scenario again and again of how and when Sallie was found dead. We compiled a list of people who needed to be questioned further. Those people included witnesses, relatives, acquaintances, neighbors, and Sallie's children. In talking with Clyde, I found out it was Sallie's four-year-old son Isaac who first reported his mommy being stabbed and killed. In fact, little Isaac witnessed the death of his mother but could not articulate or enunciate enough for anyone to take him seriously, so we thought. After seeing his mother stabbed and beaten to death, Isaac walked right out of the unlocked front door, went to the next apartment, and told Geneva Edmonds and Sallie's sister, Terri, his aunt, that his mommy would not wake up. Terri was visiting with Geneva that night and just happened to be at her apartment at the time Isaac came over. Both Geneva and Terri raced back over to Sallie's apartment where they found her body. According to Clyde, Terri said she immediately called 911 and called their father LeRue to tell him what she had witnessed.

CHAPTER 13

Diminished Glimmer of Hope

We quickly made appointments with Isaac, Terri, and her dad LeRue. I found Isaac to be the most interesting between the three, mainly because I knew he had information we wanted and needed. He was an eyewitness. I spoke with him the best I could, but I wanted to be very careful of my questioning as to not plant ideas in his head. He was the perfect witness, but I did not want any fabrication on his part, and I didn't want him to tell me something based on thoughts that I or other people painted for him. He was vulnerable, easy to lead and manipulate, and I wanted to protect him to get an accurate account of what he saw. Isaac needed professional help that we weren't prepared to give him. He needed counseling and possibly psychiatric assistance from a trained professional, and he needed it quick if we were going to get the answers we needed. The state bureau had access to experts in the field of child forensic investigations, the FBI had experts available in the field, and the police department could have provided funding for a private source if necessary. With all the resources available to us, I knew it was only a matter of time before Isaac would reveal who the killer was. Isaac had previously told Detective Woodland on the day of the murder that he saw a monster stabbing his mom in the chest with a knife. He said the monster was big with monster eyes, and he had something on the side of his sleeve near his upper shoulder. I knew Isaac could identify this monster he spoke of if he could see him again. Isaac even told

Detective Woodland that the monster had been to their house before to see his mommy.

The same day I spoke with Isaac was the same day Detective Sardoms and I approached Lieutenant Poesley about getting Isaac counseling. We both were anxious to get the counseling underway because Isaac had the key, and we were ready to unlock the door. The fire in our eyes quickly diminished like a brisk wind blowing across a lit match. Lieutenant Poesley shocked us as well as disappointed us in his response to our request. The request was not out of the box or far-fetched but very reasonable given the circumstances, but we were stopped in our tracks as we spoke to him in his office. He emphatically said, "No."

I took the lead in the conversation because I thought I had a way with the lieutenant, and I thought he trusted my judgment. I don't know what was going on in his mind the day he emphatically said no without hesitation, and he continued to be adamant about his answer and never changed his mind. I continued to express to him how imperative it was to the investigation as Detective Sardoms stood by and agreed in the background. As the lieutenant began to get even more firm about his decision, it quickly reminded me of what Clyde had told me at the forefront of the investigation, which was how the lieutenant rushed to finish the crime scene. I couldn't figure it out. Did he know this family, or did he have some animosity toward anyone in the family that I wasn't aware of? Did he think the division was so good that we would easily solve the case without outside assistance, or did he just not care? Here we were staring into the eyes of a man that spoke constantly of professionalism and getting the job done, yet he wouldn't go a step beyond to help solve this crime. He often spoke of the three *I*s of investigation he learned about somewhere in some book he read. Three *I*s of investigation: information, interrogation, and implementation. Why would he limit this investigation, and why would he see the technique of forensic interviewing as useless? I quietly searched for answers in my mind why the change in behavior, and I could only assume what was causing his opposition. The opposition only came about when I spoke of utilizing the State Bureau of Investigation. He had some negative history with a few bureau agents, thus being insulted or angered anytime the bureau was mentioned. It appeared to insult him whenever I mentioned the bureau, and even though I'm sure he was a great detective in his day, he was no match for the SBI and the resources they could provide to us in this case.

Ordinarily, his issues regarding the bureau would not faze me, but this was something different. This was a death of a young female, brutally murdered in our town, and witnessed by her own helpless child. I thought surely he would eventually agree to have the counseling done for Isaac, but he never changed his mind not even in the least bit. My opinion and my views of the lieutenant shifted somewhat that day because he put his own personal feelings in front of his duty to protect the people of Lawrence. We owed it to Isaac, we owed it to Sallie, and we owed it to Sallie's parents to do everything we possibly could to find the killer, and we were falling way short. From that day on, we didn't talk to the lieutenant much about our actions concerning this case for fear of reprisal. We just began doing what we had to do for Sallie. We had a saying around the office when we had to turn up the heat on a case, and that was it is far better to gain forgiveness than to ask for permission. I had absolutely no idea where that quote originated, but we used it quite a bit, and we still use it today. Besides, who could really be mad at us for doing the right things by just doing our jobs?

We requested the Department of Social Services to assist us with the investigation by setting up an interview with Isaac. Case workers of DSS deal with children frequently and usually have formal training when it comes to building relationships with them. The case worker agreed to set up a meeting with Isaac in a controlled and recorded room in an attempt to solicit and extract information from Isaac, but days had already passed, and his memory worsened as time went on. The session was not successful and not enough to grasp on to anything of value. It actually put us at a dead end with Isaac. It was almost like he erased the murder completely from his mind. It was definitely not the same response as the day he saw his mother killed. However, we sort of expected his memory to diminish as time passed. We just didn't know to what degree.

We interviewed Terri again who told us pretty much the same thing she reported initially. She said after Isaac told her his mommy wouldn't wake up, she immediately went to Sallie's apartment and found her dead and called 911. Although Terri was close by, she didn't see or hear anything that could help us in the case. I've got to admit though, I found her attitude and behavior to be strange. Terri was very clear and concise during her interview but didn't seem to display the feelings I would expect a close sibling to display when discussing the sudden death of her beloved sister. She spoke in detail without the slightest sign of a tear. She asked a few inquisitive questions but not many. Maybe it was her way of dealing with the situation, and maybe she had cried her last tear out of the presence of everyone else. Maybe she knew something or had some ideas locked in her head that she wasn't willing to share. Either way, I knew I wasn't satisfied with her, and I had to interview her again at a later time.

Sallie's father LeRue was next on the list. I wondered how he got to the crime scene so fast. Detective Sardoms told me he got there before any police arrived. LeRue exhibited the same behavior as his daughter Terri. He seemed concerned, but not overly concerned in my opinion. He of all people other than Sallie Hatcher's mother should have been most distraught, but he remained calm and somewhat facile while at the scene. His behavior and reactions were just as strange as Terri's. Hopefully, the weird feelings and preconceived ideas that popped in my mind were all just a figment of my imagination, and maybe I was simply dealing with a weird family. LeRue began asking basic questions like "Do you know who killed my daughter?" and "When are y'all going to make an arrest?" Although I expect those type of questions from just about anyone, it still seemed strange that it was pretty much all he asked about. Though we didn't talk a lot, LeRue did tell us that Sallie was engaged a couple of times to Ricardo, but they had separated because he didn't want to do the right thing by settling down and getting married. So she started dating someone else by the name of Jaston Setler. LeRue said he last saw his daughter about 6:00 PM the day before her death but had not seen or heard from her since. I guess LeRue told us everything he could tell us, but in the back of my mind, I knew there was something more with him also, and I would get back with him at a later time as well.

CHAPTER 14

Secrets

One day when I was in the office, I got a call from Arnita Hatcher, the girl with the Colgate smile. What she began to tell me simply astonished me but didn't surprise me. As we sat in my office and talked, Arnita told me that her sister Sallie was the victim of child molestation by their father LeRue. It was something neither of the girls dared to speak of, and Arnita told me she had not shared the story with anyone except me. Arnita was compelled to tell me because she knew LeRue could not be ruled out as one of our suspects. She told me everything and anything she could possibly think of to make sure I had all the relevant information concerning her sister, and she vowed to help me in any way she could. Like a lot of unproductive citizens who indulge in the evils of life, her father was no better, even though he was at home during their adolescent years. LeRue was also a drug abuser. Often, he would expose his children to his addiction by doing the usual things that drug abusers do. He purchased his drugs within their own neighborhood where everybody knew him and his family. He even bought drugs from Sallie and Arnita's friends and schoolmates. Many times, their friends would tell them and tease them about their drug-addict father and how he bought drugs from them. He used to steal from his own home and from his wife to support his habit. There seemed to be no boundaries when it came to supporting his habit. He sold furniture, and he worked on cars for cash to buy more drugs. Hardly ever did he take an active role in the nurturing of his daughters; however, he was quick to beat them if they stepped out of line or if they spoke to him in a manner he didn't approve of. According to the sisters, LeRue would sometimes leave and disappear for two or three days without a trace after he stole money from their mother. By accident, he frequently left the remnants of his habits behind for his family to find. He left such things as crack pipes and marijuana bags with remaining residue. Fortunately, the girls were smart enough to know that doing drugs was wrong, and they chose not to try it themselves. They knew what their daddy was doing was not good for them. Both Sallie and Arnita desperately wished their mother would leave LeRue and take them away from all the drama, but that never happened until much later.

LeRue wasn't always a freelance bum who didn't supply for his family. He was once in the United States Army and stationed at Fort Campbell, Kentucky, where he enlisted for a few years before being relieved of his duties. He was given a dishonorable discharge because even then, he was connected in some way with the drug world, and he refused to testify in a drug trial. Postmilitary, he drove interstate trucks for about a year and a half but never kept steady employment for longer than a couple of years. Typical.

LeRue was a lady's man according to his children. He was such a good father that he used to take them with him to his girlfriend's house after their mother went to work, thinking the kids were too stupid either to know or to say anything to their mother. He used to allow his women to come to their house where he would sometimes work on their cars. Arnita saw and knew a lot of things about her father that she just didn't want to talk about. Her mother was sometimes present when LeRue's lady friends would come by the house for him to work on their cars. In the years to come, the two sisters became old enough to start speaking out about LeRue's inequities, but Mrs. Adele, as we called her, rarely intervened in the altercations that took place between her husband and the girls. The only time she would intervene would be when he would beat one of the girls too hard. Other than that, their mother was just there, kind of filling a mother's space. She did matronly things and took the girls to church, but personal involvement beyond that was minuscule. There came a delicate time in the siblings' life where they came close to turning against their mother because she wouldn't intervene or acknowledge what their father was about. They seemed to think at one point that maybe their mother didn't love them or couldn't love them because she allowed them to be exposed to such dysfunctional actions by their father. Why didn't their mother take them out of that environment, especially if she knew and saw with her own eyes what her husband was doing? It was obvious to Sallie Hatcher and Arnita that their father had no real concern for their welfare, and maybe their mother didn't either. But the bond between them remained tight. Even today, Arnita wondered why their mother didn't do more at the time they needed her most. Maybe God was the only one who had the answer. Nobody else seemed to know. Even today, when Sallie's name is mentioned, or the family is reminiscing about old times, their mother shuts down and refuses to partake in the discussion. Just like Isaac, it appeared Mrs. Adele had blocked her mind of anything that involved her daughter Sallie. I'm sure she wished she had more time with her daughter, more time to let her know how much she loved her.

CHAPTER 15

Settle Up

Working in investigations sometimes gives the investigator reality checks and keeps us grounded as far as understanding people. Everything is not always as it seems. We realize that even the wealthiest person is capable of stealing, and even the prettiest can have low self-esteem because we see it all. We get a chance to see and hear things most people don't. We uncover the real stories with real people. I knew after learning everything about LeRue, he had to remain on the watch list and be interviewed again and again until we came to a conclusion. He surely could not be eliminated as his daughter's killer.

Arnita was levelheaded, smart, and focused on catching the monster that killed her sister she loved so dearly. Since LeRue had already been interviewed by the detectives on the day of the murder, I chose not to go back to him so soon for fear of him finding out he was a possible suspect. But then again, I thought how a biological father could kill his own daughter in her own house. Everybody knew LeRue, and it would be a big risk to kill Sallie. Isaac didn't mention anything about his grandfather, and no other evidence thus far had surfaced to point us in his direction. But I do know drug addicts are capable of just about anything when they are binging and scrapping for more drugs. We were interested in LeRue, but for now, Ricardo was our next target.

It was now time for us to meet with Ricardo, the baby's father and Sallie Hatcher's estranged lover, twice over. This interview had to be handled very carefully because he had a true and defined motive for killing Sallie Hatcher as I understood. Sallie had been engaged to Ricardo a couple of times but called off the wedding each time due to Ricardo's promiscuities. She had recently filed court papers seeking child support from Ricardo for his daughter Gabrella. She desperately tried to move on with her life and eventually found another lover named Jaston Setler whom Ricardo found out about and had overwhelming concern as a jealous, jilted boyfriend. Jaston was a Lawrence resident and lived only a mile from Sallie. He quickly made our suspect list, which made us work twice as hard and twice as fast. Too much time concentrated on either Ricardo or Jaston could prove to be disastrous for our case. Ricardo lived in Fayetteville, and Jaston lived in Lawrence about a mile and a half from the police department. Since it was easy for us to access Jaston, he was the suspect we chose to go after first, and we went after him hard.

After interviewing several people in the neighborhood, we found out that Jaston was in fact at Sallie's apartment the night she was killed. That by itself was not too unusual because he had been dating her. However, what was unusual was the fact that he had on a different shirt when he got off work that night before going to Sallie Hatcher's from the one he had on when he first went to work. It's common that criminals who plan their activities take on certain patterns, and one of those patterns is to decide the proper clothing to wear when the crime is committed. Once we discovered the change of shirts, thanks to the Eaton Corporation surveillance system, we knew he had to be the first one to be questioned. And since Sallie Hatcher's door was not forced open, it led us to believe the killer was no stranger. It had to be somebody she was comfortable with or intimate with because of the late hour she was killed. I would most likely believe it was an intimate partner like Jaston or Ricardo. We didn't believe it was a complete stranger because everybody we interviewed told us that Sallie never opened her door for strangers, and she pretty much kept to herself.

As an investigator, I didn't for a minute believe a stranger carved her up the way she was. This act was a vendetta, and whoever killed her wanted to punish her so bad, he posed her naked body in complete humiliation for any and everybody to see. Even though we were to interview Jaston first, in the back of my mind, the killer was Ricardo, and I was sure of it. Jaston went to Sallie Hatcher's apartment after getting off work and normally stayed for a couple of hours before his departure but never much longer. Apparently, the two of them had an understanding and a "no strings" kind of relationship. With that in mind, I wondered what Jaston's motive would be. He became less important to me as I thought about his motives or lack thereof. He really didn't have a motive. He saw her at his convenience, they socialized often, and he had no obligations to her like Ricardo. We still had to follow up on Jaston until all leads were exhausted.

Detective Sardoms and I spoke about how we would approach Jaston for the first time. We didn't completely rule him out, but he was still a suspect in the case. We came up with different conversational scenarios to prepare for an interview that could easily become an interview with a killer. Most guilty people tend to cooperate with the police as much as they possibly can to avoid suspicion or detection. It should have been an easy meeting with Jaston to ask him to come to the police department for questioning, but somehow it didn't go the way we planned. Detective Sardoms went to Jaston's house on one sunny morning as I remained at the department in preparation for the interview.

Detective Sardoms approached Jaston outside his home that day as he was at his car getting ready to go to work. Sardoms nicely requested Jaston to come to the police department for questioning, but he refused and said he didn't want to be harassed by the police according to Detective Sardoms. The detective tried to explain to Jaston that the interview was routine, and it wouldn't take very long, but Jaston refused. When Detective Sardoms returned to the department, he told me what Jaston said. I got angry at Sardoms for allowing Jaston to dictate and control the conversation in a murder case. The answer no was not an option for me, and I was hell-bent on getting some answers.

Sardoms and I got back in the car and went back to Jaston's house. This would mark the first day Jaston and I met. I was calm with him at first and wondered why he didn't want to be questioned if he wasn't guilty of anything. I'm normally very nice to people when I talk with them because it's much easier, and most people are more receptive to that type of approach. I kindly told Jaston that his name came up in the investigation and asked him why he didn't want to talk with us at the department. I assured him that once he came up and talked with us and maybe even take a polygraph exam, his name would be cleared. I told him he would not have to continue worrying about us harassing him anymore unless he was guilty of killing Sallie. I really couldn't have been much nicer. As Jaston answered my questions, he seemed somewhat squeamish as we verbally jostled back and forth. It was apparent to me that my nice-guy approach wasn't working very well with him. His attitude began to make me believe he could have something to do with the murder. All sorts of thoughts ran through my head like a whirlwind. As the winds circled, I became angrier and a bit more hostile toward Jaston. I took on those characteristics because of two reasons. First, I wondered how a young man could have a relationship with a woman and not want to assist in solving her murder if he wasn't guilty. Two, I wondered if I was talking to the killer himself. I could think of no other reason he would refuse to have a simple conversation about his whereabouts. As I held those thoughts in my head, I began to look at him like a piece of shit, and I called him that directly to his face before I could get control of myself. I told him he was shit for not wanting to cooperate in the investigation of his own girlfriend, somebody he slept with on a constant basis. I told him that he was either going to cooperate, or I was going to make his life a living hell until we closed Sallie's case. Jaston spoke with a reserved and quiet voice and didn't seem to be too insulted when I called him a piece of shit. But my aggressive alter ego got the mission accomplished. Jaston complied with my demand and agreed to meet with us at the police department.

After we met with Jaston at the police department and asked him the routine questions, I began feeling a chilling sensation as I spoke with him, and I could visualize him committing this crime. His demeanor was so cool, calm, and collective. The lack of display of emotion and his unmoved and uncaring behavior again caused me great concern. After all, we had just accused him in an indirect way of being somehow involved in his girlfriend's murder, but he showed no emotion. His demeanor was that of a person trying to hide the truth. After our line of questioning, he should have felt insulted and angry. He displayed neither characteristic. At the least, we should have seen a change in his body language, but it also remained the same. After witnessing his behavior, we asked him to submit to a polygraph as soon as possible, and he reluctantly agreed. I didn't want to press Jaston too hard for fear of him changing his mind about taking the polygraph. I knew the polygraph would lead us in the right direction. Either it would indicate Jaston as a liar, or it would eliminate him as a suspect.

On the day Jaston was to take the polygraph, I called him to make sure he would be in place. He assured me he would be at the department, but time was ticking, and there was no sign of Jaston. We started wondering what we were going to do next. We couldn't force him to take the polygraph, and we had no other evidence against him. Ten minutes late, Jaston finally walked into the department, which gave me an overwhelming feeling of relief. This was the day I was going to get my answer, and I was prepared for the worst. Detective Sardoms and I had rehearsed how we were going to attack Jaston during the interview process if he failed the polygraph. If he failed, I had no plans on letting him walk away from the department that day. Either he was going to confess to the murder, or we were going to be up all night until he told us what we needed to know.

After the testing, I was informed by the SBI polygrapher that Jaston had passed with an average score. Of course, I wanted to know what that meant and if it was conclusive, inconclusive, unable to be determined, or what. The agent explained to me that he passed but not with flying colors. He said the bureau would rather lean in favor of the suspect and the side of caution when results were questionable. That was certainly not what I wanted to hear. To me, however, that meant Jaston failed, and it simply meant he was a good liar. I allowed Jaston to go home after the polygraph, but I wasn't satisfied nor was I finished with him.

The next day, I asked Sardoms to return to Jaston's house again and asked him to submit to a blood analysis, better known as a DNA sample. Again, he told Detective Sardoms no. He was not going to submit to any more tests, and again, I got angry. I was determined to get what I wanted from Jaston whether he liked it or not or whether he was guilty or innocent, but I had to close this chapter one way or another. It was a couple of weeks later that I went back to Jaston's house to get him to comply, but his mother informed me he had transferred to Rocky Mount, North Carolina, with his job, and he was now living there. How odd was it that his girlfriend got killed and he quickly moved out of town? How convenient was that? His relocating put my curiosity and suspicions at an all-time high and made me want to crucify him and even start to despise him.

We got a judge to sign a search warrant to secure a DNA sample from Jaston, and Detective Sardoms and I went to Rocky Mount in search for Jaston. Jaston had no idea we would show up at his workplace, and we definitely caught him off guard as his supervisor brought him into the office where we were waiting. His eyes were in disbelief and of embarrassment, which was actually the reaction I expected and wanted. Jaston needed to know that we weren't going to accept his bullshit, and he needed to know we meant business.

We took him into custody at his workplace and in front of his coworkers and transported him to the nearest medical facility in order to draw a blood sample. Jaston was his normal self. He only asked how we knew where to find him. I gave him vague answers and continued on our journey. After we got the blood sample, we took him back to work, and we returned to Lawrence. A good day's work had been done. Now was a time for praying and waiting for the results. Even though I initially thought Ricardo was our prime suspect, my focus turned strongly toward Jaston because of all the negative energy generated from him and his sudden move to Rocky Mount.

Somehow, I managed yet again to find myself in another compromised position. During this time, I was dating a young lady from Rockingham, North Carolina named Terrida who was closely related to Jaston. I had no idea she was related to him, but she quickly let me know after her family blasted me for questioning Jaston. Her family got to know me pretty well and liked me until they found out I was the drive behind Sallie's investigation. Jaston had told them everything he had to go through, and I'm sure he told them about our somewhat-less-than-friendly conversations and meetings. The family often called my girlfriend to engage her in a conversation about the case and express to her their concern with my attitude and the way I went about doing things. I had no idea my girlfriend was part of Jaston's family, not that it made any difference, but it would have been nice to know. Of course, my girlfriend showed me nothing but loyalty and refused to go into any details about the case or talk negatively about me. However, I'm sure it didn't make her feel good, and it caused some disconcertment between her and the family. We suffered a lot of frustration throughout this case, and this was one that I wished I could have avoided. But after all that, it didn't much matter because we broke up and went our separate ways anyway. After the sample DNA was taken, our mission was complete for the time being, and we could go no further with him until the results came back. It was now time for us to go after Ricardo, our other prime suspect, the father of Sallie Hatcher's three-year-old son. Indeed, we did go after Ricardo, and just like Jaston's case, we went after him hard.

CHAPTER 16

The Usual Suspect

The investigation of Ricardo Delsado began. We couldn't dig up much on Ricardo because most of his family were not able to be reached. Those that were able to be reached didn't really know much about Ricardo or the murder. Close contact was something that didn't exist in his family. He was somewhat distant with most of his relatives and somewhat of a loner until he got together with his fraternity brothers. Whenever he got with them, he seemed to be a different person altogether according to his frat brothers. The best way to get information about a person was to talk to those closest to him. In Ricardo's case, that would be the fraternity brothers of Alpha Psi Alpha. Although Ricardo was a student at Fayetteville State University, he had very close ties with the brothers at the University of Pembroke. I never found out why that was the case, but it really didn't matter because these were his boys. The common code of fraternities is to protect their brothers no matter what the cost. I'm sure that code is taken seriously by those who pledge, but I knew once we talked about murder and conspiracy to a bunch of college undergrads, the code could easily be broken. Well, I was right again. Sure, the few we spoke with who saw Ricardo on the day of the murder tried to be tough but soon broke down and told us the times and places they saw and were with him. They admitted to being with him and even told us what they watched on television. They confirmed a story Ricardo told earlier about being in a wrestling match and about the time he left Fayetteville State where they all hung out after the match. So much for the code. We had no idea whether the information would be useful or not at the time, but it certainly closed the gap on time and assisted in providing a time line that we would later need at the conclusion of our investigation. After we spoke to the frat brothers, there was nobody else left to tell us anything else about Ricardo other than Ricardo himself.

Detective Sardoms and I drove to Fayetteville, North Carolina, the home of Fort Bragg, one of the largest military institutions in the United States and home of the Eighty-Second Airborne Battalion, Green Berets or Special Forces. Not too far away from the soldiers who protect our country was a possible killer who lived in Seacrest Apartments on Carmen Street. It was in Carmen Street apartments where we found Ricardo living in his current girlfriend's two-bedroom apartment. We caught Ricardo by surprise that day as he didn't think we would travel to Fayetteville just to speak to him. After all, he refused our invitation on a couple of prior occasions claiming he was too busy. We were most glad to accommodate and make it easy for him as we met him at the door while his girlfriend watched in somewhat of a baffled look.

I'm sure she had never had the police come to her apartment before to question anyone about a murder. We didn't want to embarrass her any more than we had to, but we wanted both her and Ricardo to know we meant business, and we would not stop until finished. We were gentle with Ricardo only because we both knew we didn't have any evidence on him, and if we took a hard approach, he would probably clam up or hire a lawyer like most guilty people do. Even though our dialogue with him was gentle, we got very intrusive with him, and he answered most of our questions. This guy was supercool and really not even mad that we were at his home questioning him as a possible suspect. That action by itself or lack thereof was enough for me to have my suspicions. After questioning him at his home, we requested he meet us at the police department where he would feel a little less comfortable.

A couple of days had passed by, and the time finally came when we interviewed Ricardo at the police station. Not only did we interview him, we asked him to submit to a polygraph examination and a blood analysis to extract DNA. He cooperated fully with the interview and granted our requests for the tests. He complied very easily with no resistance at all, although I expected a small degree of resistance, which is usually typical of those who are deceptive or guilty. Ricardo had answers for all our questions and had pretty good-sounding excuses, but we continued to drill him and close every possible alibi we could think of. Getting all the details on his alibis were very important because if he was lying, we could tear his story apart, and it would surely bring him closer into focus. Everybody knows if you tell the truth, the truth can be told again and again, and nothing would change. But a lie is something totally different. One lie compounds another and another, and things would surely change a little more every time it's told. Listening and taking meticulous notes were a must when it came to talking to Ricardo, and we did just that. We interviewed him for at least three hours that day in Detective Sardoms's office. After the interview was over, he looked exhausted but somewhat relieved that he could leave with a promise to return for a polygraph.

Ricardo did in fact return as he said he would to take the polygraph given by the North Carolina State Bureau of Investigation. A makeshift room was already set up for the session to be held. We normally drive to Fayetteville to get the polygraphs done at the bureau office, but the bureau was just as interested in solving the murder as we were, so they obliged us in any way they could, including coming to Lawrence to do the polygraphs. After about an hour, Ricardo appeared downstairs of the police department, which is usually indicative of test being completed or terminated for some other reason. As Ricardo continued out the front door, I told him I would be in touch with him at a later time. He had no idea if he passed the polygraph or not. It was not a practice to tell the person taking the test if he or she passed or failed. That decision is left up to the investigator in charge of the case, and of course, we didn't tell. Detective Sardoms and I went upstairs to get the results and were astonished to find out Ricardo passed the test. A moment of silence came between us, and a cloud of frustration filled the room. We were positive Ricardo would fail. He was our prime suspect. My ego took a dive that day, and my gas wasn't as potent as it normally was after I got that devastating news, but we had to keep pressing on. We had to get the truth, and we weren't willing to settle for an unsolved mystery. I didn't have an explanation for Ricardo's successful score on the polygraph, but I was taught to go where the facts led me, and the fact at hand was that he passed the test. Maybe, just maybe, he didn't kill Sallie, and maybe the killer was still lurking among us. Although we stopped badgering Ricardo, it didn't keep us from plastering posters around college campuses and talking with students in hopes of meeting someone who could tell us something useful. Meeting that someone never came to fruition, and it was time to close the book on Ricardo.

CHAPTER 17

Lost in Time

It seemed like once we closed the book on Ricardo, Sallie's case seemed to become less and less important to the division as time went on. Other cases were building up and had to be dealt with. I guess that would be looking at it from a managerial perspective, because to me, nothing else existed other than solving Sallie's murder. I could see Detective Sardoms's enthusiasm debilitating as well, but I knew Clyde was sincere about the case, but just like me, he didn't have any answers and not too many places to go. Sallie's case made somewhat of a spectacle out of the police department and put us in an embarrassing light among the community. People started talking about us and asking questions on a regular basis. We gave a lot of generic answers, knowing full well we didn't have any answers for them. To save myself some embarrassment and humiliation, I took a coward's approach and often referred questions asked by the community to Detective Sardoms since he was the lead investigator. I was not prepared to tell anyone that we were at ground zero and didn't have a clue as to who committed this awful crime in the midst of our city. It was an awkward position to be in, especially for me, because our victim was black, the murder happened in the heart of the black community, and I was the black face of the police department whom the black population in Lawrence was familiar with in some way or form.

The black community was looking for me to connect with them, keep them informed, and simply help them in their time of bereavement and terror. I began to feel more and more isolated from my own people as the department began to isolate them. Usually, day-to-day people always have questions to ask, sometimes because they just wanted to talk, and at other times, they were just simply being nosy. This time, it was different. A lot of people knew Sallie and her family, and they were asking out of concern for them, but most of all, I believe others were asking out of fear for their own lives and safety because every female was a potential victim. The questions were understandable and acceptable as a killer was still roaming the streets of Lawrence, and nobody had a clue to who this person may be. We desperately needed help, and we had reached out to any and every one we thought could help in some shape, form, or fashion. We spoke to teachers, pastors, fraternities, police officers, factory workers, the unemployed, and even the vagrants who were often considered menaces to society. We even had a two-minute segment on the television series *Carolina's Most Wanted*, and still, we had nothing.

There came a time when I became angry with the black community because I felt like I was carrying the weight of the people on my shoulders. Even though the chief of police was black and the lieutenant of detectives was black, there was a definite lack of pressure to resolve this case both from inside the department and eventually from the outside as well. I guess the disconcertment came because the case seemed to be getting old or better known as stale. Nobody seemed to be doing enough in my opinion in regard to scrutinizing the investigation or keeping it to the forefront. I knew firsthand how other people would call and complain to the police department about their concerns and quickly get resolution. But for some reason, blacks in the community didn't make it a habit of making such calls and allowed things to go unnoticed. When they did call, our assistance seemed to be less than that of our counterparts. Therefore, our problems sometimes continued without ever being addressed or resolved.

I thought what happened to Sallie would make a difference, but it didn't. Calls of concern were far and few outside Sallie's family whom I've gained much respect for during such a traumatic time. They called sometimes weekly to get updates or at least make a connection with anyone they could to get some answers about the case. Arnita met me at the police department several times just to talk about the case. It was easy to tell that she was the strongest and most logical person within the family, and she was someone I could talk to freely and without repercussions. I even shared a few things about the case that I shouldn't have, but she never once compromised our trust between each other. She simply took in the information in hopes it would help her recollect something in her sister's past that would be beneficial in the case.

She too knew that enough wasn't being done to solve her sister's murder and asked me for guidance. Again, I found myself in an awkward position because I was loyal to the department and to my work. But I also owed loyalty to Sallie. How could I be loyal to both when both factions were clearly divided? I finally suggested to Arnita and her family to bypass the police department and request a meeting with the mayor and city manager. At the meeting, the family was to express their dissatisfaction with the police investigation, the lack of interest, and their dismay about not being kept informed of new developments in the case. I didn't see Arnita for days after that, but it was obvious the meeting had taken place. The case gained new life within the department, and we were instructed to go back in the neighborhoods and interview residents. We put up more posters and held roadblocks to distribute information as well as to acquire it from motorists. Wow, just one simple meeting was able to change the course and renew the investigation. Even though it maybe was not a sincere action on our part, it was being done, which was the main objective.

I found the roadblocks to be most beneficial in that it gave the community a chance to see us working for them in their own neighborhoods. We got a chance to talk to a lot of residents and give them some sense of security. I saw quite a few people out just walking, which was something they had not been comfortable doing for a while. Several traffic citations were written on the evening of the roadblock, and several warrants were served after suspects were spotted in somebody's car during the roadblocks. Juvenile investigator Daryl Wilcox was also helping out with our efforts. Daryl probably knew about 95 percent of the population, both white and black. He was well liked and respected among the community in which he was born and bred. People hated to see Daryl Wilcox because he would frequently identify them as someone who had outstanding warrants, and they knew he would be the cause of them getting locked up.

It was nothing special when Investigator Wilcox who everybody knows simply as Dal spotted a guy named Toby Singleton in the passenger side of a friend's car that night. Dal called me on the police radio and told me he just saw Toby, but when Toby saw him, he got out of the car and walked away. Dal asked me if I wanted him to stop him, and I told him yes. I was sure Toby was either drunk or had a warrant on him. Besides, he was also the guy lingering around the neighborhood on the day Sallie was killed. Dal said he quickly tried to catch up with Toby, but he disappeared into the night. He told me he thought Toby went into one of the apartments, but he couldn't be sure. We didn't have a great concern about catching Toby because our only real focus was catching the killer. We continued with the roadblock for another hour and called it quits with nothing new to report.

CHAPTER 18

North Meets South

Time passed by, and we still had no strong suspects, and we rarely did anything to cultivate any until one day when I saw an older black man walk into the police department and into Lieutenant Poesley's office. I saw the chief come and go out of the lieutenant's office as well. I had no idea who this tall, strong stature of a man was, but he was wearing a very nice-looking business suit and sounded most polite with a slight accent. I felt his presence and importance as I watched him from across the hall. He walked in Lieutenant Poesley's office, and the door closed behind him, but I was soon to find out the identity of this polished and well-mannered but unusual man.

I served in many capacities within the police department, and on this day, I was in the evidence vault performing evidence-control tasks. Our evidence technician had resigned from the department to take a higher-paying job with fewer demands. The vault was located only about eight feet and right in front of the lieutenant's door, which allowed me to hear just about everything as I stood there. It was not like I was snooping and listening to conversations, but the lieutenant was fully aware that I could possibly hear conversations from the vault because of its proximity. I was a trusted employee, and nobody seemed to mind me being in the know. In fact, both the lieutenant and the chief discussed a lot of classified information with me. Apparently, the meeting was a jovial one because I heard periodic laughter and friendly dialogue, but I couldn't hear enough to decipher the conversation.

As the door to the lieutenant's office opened, they all emerged from the room, and I assumed they walked the gentleman to the door, which is something we normally do for anyone visiting on business. Soon after the gentleman's departure, the chief handed me a check for $25,000 and told me to place it in the vault for safekeeping. The check was a reward to anyone with information leading to the arrest of Sallie Hatcher's killer. The check was given to the chief by the unidentified suited gentleman who had just left the building. The man was Clyburn Gray, Sallie's long-lost grandfather she never knew existed. And like Sallie, he knew nothing of her existence until her death. Neither the chief nor the lieutenant talked about this man called Gray, and I wondered why. We often talked among each other in the division, but this time, it seemed to be a different aura in the air. The chief told me Mr. Gray was Sallie's grandfather, but the conversation quickly diminished beyond that, and no other real information was shared with me, except that it was Gray who put up the reward money. I placed the check in the vault and thought to myself that Mr. Gray must have known a lot of people to collect so much money. It didn't matter where he got the money from though because it was the greatest break we had in the case in a while, and I was glad to get it. Surely, someone would surface with this kind of loot available.

Lawrence was not a town full of prominent blacks, and I found it to be odd, a miracle, and a blessing all at the same time that someone cared enough about this case to put up that kind of money. In the back of my mind, I assumed that Mr. Gray was the front person for a group of people who collected money for the cause. It was hard for me to conceive a black man from Lawrence was solely responsible for such a large amount of money. Lawrence was not full of wealthy people, but there was still something about this man that just didn't fit the mold.

After all my thoughts went racing everywhere about Mr. Gray, I did find out that he was in fact the sole interest bearer on the $25,000. It was his money from his own personal account. He asked for nothing in return other than to find his granddaughter's killer. How noble, how unselfish, and how sublime I thought of the gesture.

CHAPTER 19

The Neighborhood

I got excited after learning of the reward and the origin from which it came but yet angry because I had suggested a reward early in the investigation when I thought information could be obtained and when the time was most crucial. But I was ignored as usual when it came to increasing our efforts in the case. Not many people knew the level of my compassion and my commitment in Sallie Hatcher's case, and I tried not to let it overtake me. I controlled my emotions the best I could, but everyone needs that one person to talk to. My person was Daryl, the juvenile investigator. He seemed to be the only other person who could really understand the struggle encountered throughout this case. He too witnessed firsthand how nonchalant everybody was including our department leaders. During this time, there were only seven black officers within a department of forty-five. Of course, I knew everyone in the department, and I was aware of the limited number of black influence within the organization, but even the other blacks didn't understand the struggle. Even they went on with their routine activities like Sallie's murder wasn't a big deal. None of them ever even bothered to ask how the case was going or if we had any suspects or if they could help in some way. Sure, I was disappointed in the department as a whole, but I was highly disappointed in my own people because I expected more from them, because Sallie was one of us.

Daryl was my only sounding board whom I could really confide in and open up a candid conversation with. He seemed to understand the constant struggle we had when it came to our own race. It always seemed like an uphill battle for us to get justice the way our counterparts received it. He and I talked almost daily as we still do today, and I appreciated him to no end because he was true to who he was, but yet he was also true to the people. It was only because he understood the struggle and became part of it that he also gave special attention to our African American community. Neither of us would enjoy being called racist, and we didn't consider ourselves as such, but there was no choice other than to take notice of the distinction between the two cultures when it came to police services. We learned a lot about ourselves during this time, and it was Sallie who brought us closer than we have ever been. The department's response forced Daryl and I to sometimes go beyond the call of duty to help other less fortunate people; race didn't matter, but we felt like we had to give special attention to the black community because they needed representation, a voice, and someone they could trust for help.

It was about six months since Sallie Hatcher's death, and it seemed like we were back at square one. Jaston Setler's DNA results came back negative as did Ricardo's. Closing the case was something we were not ready to do.

Another neighborhood canvass was performed, which was when officers physically went door to door and ask neighborhood residents questions pertaining to the investigation. The questions were very general but specific in nature. The questions were trigger questions and could lead to a more in-depth conversations if any positive responses were elicited. To the untrained ear, the questions were viewed as just general-type questions. But to the investigator, the questions were calculated and meant to solicit information without alerting the person being questioned. The questions allow us to quickly examine the person interviewed, their families and friends. It is imperative that we listen carefully because we could have very well been interviewing a friend of the killer, the killer's family, or ultimately, the killer himself.

We got a chance to interview several people who had interesting backgrounds, which made me realize how vulnerable a city can be, almost at the mercy of the criminal elements. One of the interesting folks was Charlie Pounds. He lived just around the corner from Sallie, but little did anybody in the neighborhood knew that he was a convicted murderer from the state of New York. We discovered he was convicted of murder when we checked backgrounds of males living in the surrounding area. He killed his girlfriend, did time in prison, and moved to Lawrence where he lay low and stayed below the radar. What was a convicted murderer doing in our midst, in our neighborhood, in our faces every day, living a normal life? We questioned Pounds after we caught him off guard outside his apartment washing his car. We asked to speak to him inside, and he obliged us in a somewhat-reluctant manner. Almost like he thought we were coming to get him, which struck me as suspicious. Two police detectives approached him, asked to talk to him inside his apartment, and he didn't even ask why. Yes, I was really suspicious.

We had a brief conversation with him, and he gave us short and somewhat evasive answers. I made sure I asked him questions that he should have had the answers to but didn't. I asked him questions like, Did you hear about what happened to Sallie Hatcher? His response was, "No more than she was killed." I asked him who told him about the murder. His response was, "Just somebody in the neighborhood." We played this cat-and-mouse game for about thirty minutes, and I knew this guy had to be checked out a little further. He was placed on our watch list, and after checking him through the Division of Criminal Information Network, otherwise known as DCI, we then discovered that he was a convicted murderer. Not only was he a murderer, he was a murderer who was from another state, a murderer who lived only several yards behind Sallie Hatcher and could easily blend in the night as he watched her comings and goings. He could literally see the back of her house from the front of his patio, which could be taunting for any sexual deviant. For those reasons alone, Pounds moved to the top of our suspect list.

The more we canvassed the neighborhood, the more we found about the lives of people in the community. Strange things were told to us by a few, and a lady who lived just down the street told a story that was no exception. Her name was Ernestine. She told me about a black mailman who used to deliver mail to her apartment in the year 2001. She didn't know if he delivered mail to Sallie's apartment or not, but she told me he made special efforts to come and visit her during his route. She said the mailman would come to her apartment after business hours to have conversation with her and often talked about having sex. Somehow and for some crazy reason, I knew there had to be more to this story than she was leading us to believe, but we continued to give her our undivided attention. She said he tried several times to get her to have sex with him, but she repeatedly refused his advances.

After he realized he wasn't getting anywhere with her, he threatened to tell some nasty things about her to the pastor of her church. He knew all about her because she thought she could trust him and confided in him about some of the deepest things in her life. She didn't want him to spoil her good name, and she felt trapped, according to her, and eventually let him have his way. As we continued to listen to her story, she became increasingly believable, and I became absorbed in her perilous scandal. I could start to see the disgust and anguish as she spoke, and not only did I feel sorry for what she had been through, but I felt sorry for the other woman who had to be subjected to his behavior of entrapment. Ernestine had been mentally raped. She believed she was raped but was embarrassed to tell anyone about her dreadful stupidity. She didn't think anyone would believe her, and she kept the ordeal locked inside her until the day she told us the story.

As absurd as it may seem and no matter how intellectual and reputable she was, she was right when she wondered who would believe her. Even I didn't at first. But we knew we had to pursue this mailman she spoke of. Just like Charlie Pounds, the mailman didn't live in Lawrence either. However, if she was telling the truth, we had another dangerous man lurking in our city and preying on our defenseless women. If she was telling the truth, this could be the break that we had been waiting for. The mailman was added to our watch list right beneath Charlie Pounds.

Although the story she told us was unusual, it seemed to somewhat fit the puzzle as to why we were not able to solve the mystery. Everything we were told about these potential murders fell right into place as the typical loner-type personalities. They were not natives of the area, and hardly anyone knew them, which allowed them to slither about the neighborhoods undetected. How could anyone reveal any information about these people when nobody knew them or associated with them? She described the mailman as somewhat muscular, which could be why he was able to overtake his victim. He preyed upon single women he knew he could easily overtake, like Ernestine and Sallie.

After checking his work history, we found out he was a troublemaker in the workplace also and often exhibited a bad attitude when he couldn't get his way. He was flirtatious and even went as far as slapping a coworker on the ass much to her dismay. To me, this would be the type of guy who enjoyed demoralizing women and viewed women as less than deserving. After receiving this information from Ted's supervisor, I had to ask him why he continued to let someone like Ted remain with the agency. The answer I got was short and simple: Ted was unionized and was untouchable at the time. It was a travesty and disgraceful to allow a man to continue to work and demoralize and degrade women. If I had my way, he would have been fired and locked behind bars, but lucky for us, he was still employed, and he wasn't hard to find at all.

We made a few cautious and secretive attempts to find Ted because we wanted to catch him by surprise. We wanted him unprepared and unrehearsed. It's hard for people to answer questions when they are not prepared, and it's easy to tell when they attempt to be deceptive, misleading, or simply telling lies. We finally caught up with him and rigorously questioned him at a local police station. After interviewing him for a couple of hours about his former mail route in Tara Village, it too became apparent that this was not our killer either. His answers somewhat coincided with Ernestine's, but there was also a level of sincerity in his voice about his promiscuous actions with her. Astonishing enough, he came right out with the answers with little provocation. He literally told us just about everything told by Ernestine. The only difference was she was more of a willing participant, and he merely took advantage of her mental incompetence and low self-esteem. We terminated yet another interview without any results whatsoever, and our hope continued to get more and more dismal.

I felt helpless, and I felt like I didn't know where to turn or who to turn to. We had suspects, but that's all we had suspects and nothing more, but I was not ready to give up. Instead, I became even more consumed with Sallie Hatcher, hoping I would be the one to crack the case. I was sort of drawn to the big cases, and I enjoyed the spotlight and the notoriety it brought after cases were successfully closed and cleared. Lieutenant Poesley often joked with me about wanting the spotlight, but he was always pleased with my work and the results of it.

My comrades had never seen me work so diligently until Sallie's death. They started teasing me during staff meetings, asking me sarcastically if I ever slept with Sallie Hatcher. I would usually manage to muster up no more than a smile after the silly comments to avoid the frustration of dealing with ignorance and the feeling of separatism when it came to cultural and racial disparities. To me, this case wasn't one to be joked about, and the office clownery and banter I had the privilege of hearing was never forgotten. I guess I surprised my counterparts by my newfound behavior they just couldn't get used to. I was always the jovial one in the bunch, and I always had smiles, laughter, and words of encouragement on a daily basis. So maybe the ribbing I got from the guys should have been expected, but then again, they should have respected my sincerity in the process.

CHAPTER 20

Clyburn Gray

As the weeks went by with no progress, I heard more and more rumors from the streets. The rumors were again about the man named Clyburn Gray. The word on the street was that he was related to Sallie Hatcher, and he was possibly her long-lost grandfather. I couldn't believe the streets because the information was too far-fetched. It couldn't be true in my mind because Sallie Hatcher and her family had no money. They were poor financially and never had any other resources other than themselves. Clyburn Gray was a multimillionaire, I heard. Of course, everyone knows that in small towns, word travels fast, but only a few select people knew the real truth. My chief was one of those people who usually knew the real truth. He confirmed everything I heard. Clyburn Gray was, in fact, Sallie Hatcher's grandfather. Sallie's mother was his long-lost daughter that he never knew existed. It was then that I began to understand the $25,000 reward. He wanted to help find the person responsible for killing his granddaughter. But was this a reward based on guilt, one based on boasting and ego tripping, or was he genuine in his efforts? It wasn't for me to figure out, and I was just glad the reward was offered. Sadly, even though the reward was offered and we saturated the community with information about the reward, nobody came forward.

  Months later with no results, Mr. Gray rescinded his offer. On the day the offer was rescinded, I watched him come into the police department and go into Lieutenant Poesley's office again along with the chief. I was in my office at the time, so I couldn't hear any of the conversation, but I desperately wondered what was being said. I quickly found out when the lieutenant came to my office and told me to get the check out of the vault and said sternly, "The man wants his check back." I didn't ask any questions. I got the check, handed it to the lieutenant as requested, and later found out that day the reward was no longer offered. The lieutenant told me Mr. Gray wanted to find another way of finding Sallie's killer, and he didn't think the reward was serving its purpose. As he told me this, I already knew the ugly truth. The truth was that Mr. Gray was treated just like any regular John Doe from the streets when he came into the department, hoping to get some answers about his granddaughter's case. Instead of getting answers and quality conversation, he got short, evasive answers from both the chief and the lieutenant. I was told that he felt insulted and did not want any more dealings with the police department because we didn't seem to care or have sympathy for what happened to Sallie Hatcher. I wished I could have talked with him before his impressions were solidified because I did care, and I wanted closure to the case just as much as he. But I didn't get the opportunity, at least not at that time.

Lots of townsfolk started talking about a new restaurant that opened within the Ramada Inn Motel. I heard many say how good the food was and that it was one of the better buffets in the area. Well, it was me and Clyde's turn to go one Thursday. We talked about restaurants and good food often when we worked together and exchanged interesting recipes for the grill. Of course, we couldn't pass up the restaurant hoopla that was going around about the new place within the Ramada Inn. I could smell the fried chicken outside, and it smelled so good. As we approached the front door, we saw people coming and going without dally as they headed for the buffet meal. This place had to be good with the clientele I saw going in. Teachers, lawyers, government employees, and more. I could never have imagined what Clyde and I were about to walk into as the next moment almost devastated us both.

As we walked into the front entrance, we were greeted by no other than Adele Hatcher, Sallie Hatcher's mother! She was dressed in very swanky clothes, which complemented her from what I was used to seeing. Her hair had new bounce and luster, and even her talk was something I wasn't used to. It was like she went through a complete metamorphosis. She greeted us with a wonderful smile and acknowledged both of us individually. "Welcome to the Clyburn Inn," she said, and we followed her to the dining area. Her walk was even different. A new sway and a new swagger is what I saw. Although it was nice to see her, I was confused as to what was wrong with her or what went right. I wondered if she had a nervous breakdown, and this was the result. I wondered if this was the way she was coping with her tragedy. I wondered if she could even stand to look at me or Clyde, knowing her daughter's murder had not been solved. I could have bought Clyde for a penny that day as he was just as confused as I. He was embarrassed and felt a feeling of despair because he was in charge of the case. It was hard for him to make eye contact with Mrs. Hatcher because he felt like he failed her, her entire family, and most of all, he felt like he failed Sallie Hatcher. After we were seated at a table, Clyde found it hard to eat. He struggled with his emotions as he kept shaking his head from side to side, saying he felt so bad. I knew his pain because I was going through it with him. Neither of us knew what was racing through Mrs. Hatcher's mind because she only lightly mentioned the case. She only asked if we had any leads as she led us to our table. In my opinion, she could have done without seeing either of us, but we could never tell by the greeting we received. Hopefully, it was divine intervention that allowed her to greet and treat us so gracefully. Either way it was, I was glad to see her working, getting out of the house and smiling again.

 As weeks continued to pass by, the streets started talking again, and the news was simply astonishing and found to be true. The rich black man who bought the Ramada Inn was Clyburn Gray; thus, the name the Clyburn Inn was born. Since I'm one who checks resources, I checked once more with those whom I knew would have the right information. Both the chief and the lieutenant confirmed that Clyburn Gray purchased the Ramada Inn and the property surrounding it. They told me he paid well over one million dollars for the property. *My god*, I thought to myself. How divine and awesome

God was to bring such a spirited gentleman to a town of turmoil and unrest. Not only was Mr. Gray Sallie Hatcher's grandfather, he was now a legitimate business owner of a major chain motel. Not only that, he literally took his daughter from a desolate and dark place in her life and gave her new life. My questions were all answered the day I found out that Mr. Gray was the sole owner of the Ramada Inn, which shortly thereafter changed the name to the Clyburn Inn. Mrs. Adele Hatcher was now working for her own father, the multimillionaire. How awesome was that?

It seemed like overnight the Hatcher family was swept away and rushed into a place they could only have dreamed about. New cars were purchased for all the granddaughters along with a new house, which was located on the other side of town and close to the Clyburn Inn. I'm sure the house purchase was a strategic move made by Mr. Gray. He kept his daughter close and wanted her close to the business to keep a watchful eye on the day-to-day activities. I found myself somewhat overwhelmed with joy to witness such a beautiful thing, and to actually know the people involved made it even more joyous. Sallie's death brought about life, a life she will never get to experience, but a life for her family and her children. Her entire family will have no more burdens like the ones they had throughout their life. Isaac's and Gabrella's life would be changed forever!

It was a Tuesday morning when I was at my office doing routine work and going about my day as normal. It wasn't a real busy day for me, and nothing out of the ordinary happened that day except for the phone call I received from Arnita Hatcher. It was good to hear her jovial and pleasant voice. We exchanged pleasantries as we normally did, but just by the phone call, I could tell she had been transformed just as her mother was. Her talk was totally different than the last time I spoke to her, and she never spoke of the case at all but called me on a business proposition. I was so proud of her. Even though I only spoke to her over the phone, I knew she was coping well with her loss and coping with where the investigation was, which was nowhere. Arnita told me that the Clyburn Inn was contracting different bands to come and play at the establishment, and she was interested in security options. Off-duty security for officers was twenty-five dollars per hour with a minimum of three hours. She didn't seem to mind the rate and acted as it wasn't a problem at all. I guess I was the one who had to get used to the transformation. She seemed to be doing fine. Arnita told me she would be getting back up with me at a later time about the different dates that security would be needed. She said she really wanted me to be part of the security team because she knew me, and I was recommended to her by other hosts. I suggested she speak with the chief if she specifically wanted me as part of the team, which was just a formality. I had no reason to think the chief would deny her request. She quickly did exactly as suggested. The chief gave me the okay, and dates were set.

That night finally came, and I saw Arnita again for the first time in a long time. Like her mother, she looked great! She had on a well-fitted flowery dress with two-inch heels. Her hair had a free flow to it, much like hair that had been freshly permed. And she too had that sway to her walk, just like her mother. Again, I couldn't believe my eyes. When I looked at her, I saw a woman who was perfectly housed in a plain but seducing dress. My assumptions resurfaced when I saw her. It had to be her coping mechanism. Nobody could transform so fast and do it so well with such a devastation lingering in the background. But then again, maybe it was just me again who hadn't come to terms with the whole ordeal or could accept it. There were three other private security members already on site upon my arrival. They were given strict instructions on who was in charge of security for the night, and that was me. The security team was out of Fayetteville and well established, so there wasn't a lot of instruction that had to be given. We all seemed to mesh well, and we all understood our roles, which made it comfortable for me and somewhat safe when it came to communication. Not that trouble was expected, but we had to prepare for the inevitable. Anytime there is a room full of people, music, and alcohol, a fight or two is bound to happen, or three or maybe even four.

Arnita and I talked every chance we got during the night, and she told me all about the plans she had for the nightclub named CG's. She was as excited as I've ever seen her, and I was surely glad to see that pretty smile again as she spoke to me about her granddaddy who purchased the establishment of which we were all employed. I thought it was the greatest thing to happen as she spoke but yet the strangest thing. Why didn't Mr. Gray do something for his family before Sallie Hatcher's death? I wondered. In other words, why did it take a member of his family to die before he acted on their behalf? I would never have asked such a crude question to anyone, but Arnita clarified it for me without even knowing she did. She told me that it was Sallie Hatcher's death that got the attention of the grandfather she too never knew. She told me that somehow, he learned of his family through a friend who resided in Lawrence, and once he confirmed the information through the work of a private investigator, he came to Lawrence and wanted to do something for the family he never knew. He bought the motel, bought them cars, houses, and put the entire Hatcher family in charge of motel operations. Just like that.

    As I stayed connected with the establishment, I saw Mrs. Hatcher's new car, I saw Arnita's new car, and I saw the new home Mrs. Hatcher moved into along with the property she acquired. Jamaya was also working at the motel as part of the management. Everybody was working in their own family-owned business. Gifts were bestowed on to the entire family, and the Hatchers quickly became elitists of Lawrence. Not only did the family get a fresh start and a makeover, but so did the motel. What was once known as a run-down Ramada Inn Motel where hardly anyone with any class would stay the night quickly became a prime piece of property after renovations and reconstruction were finished. The grounds were well landscaped with greenery that stretched from the front to the back. The pool was clean and refurbished and added even more attractiveness to the area. Even though the rooms had no inside corridors, there was still a sense of safety because security was hired, lights and video equipment were installed, and rooms were refurbished and refurnished. The atrium of the motel was a grand entrance, complete with an elegant chandelier, large flat-screen television, plush couches and chairs, and designer decor. Banquet halls were rented out often, and nobody seemed to mind the steep price charged for the rental. One of my favorites of the establishment was of course

CG's Steakhouse. I continued to go there for lunch and sometimes dinner. The food was always fresh and good to my palate. I could tell that I wasn't the only one with this type of sentiment as I saw lots of the same faces when I frequented the restaurant, and it was the talk around town when it came to good food. This was truly a rags-to-riches fairy-tale life.

Even though things were looking well for the Hatcher family and their focus seemed to diminish from the police department, the murder of Sallie Hatcher was still unsolved, and there was still a monster lurking somewhere within our city. Clyburn Gray had not forgotten that, and he never lost focus of his purpose of existence. I received a phone call one day from Mr. Gray's daughter, Adele. She called me on my cell phone on behalf of Mr. Gray and wanted to set up a time that I could meet with her father to discuss business, I assume. She never told me why Mr. Gray wanted to see me, but I assumed he wanted to beef up security around the motel. I met with him a couple of days after the phone call and found out it wasn't about security at all. I was honored, nervous, and a bit apprehensive about meeting the millionaire of a man because I was sure we had nothing in common other than the business of security. I had never met a millionaire to my knowledge, so this was truly something different for me. Not only was he a millionaire, he was a millionaire several times over. He had power, influence, but yet humble in my opinion because he didn't have to be in Lawrence. He could have been anywhere in the world, but he chose little Lawrence to build his small empire and build wealth for his family.

I had no idea what I was going to say to Mr. Gray upon meeting him, and I surely didn't want to disappoint him. I found myself practicing how I would greet him. A handshake with a formal voice and a business-style look or a handshake and a smile. After I went over the ritual a few times, I realized how silly I was being, and with that in mind, I decided to be myself without any fronting and no preconceived notions on who the man was that I was about to meet. The Thursday evening of the meeting finally came, but it was a day that I had my eight-year-old son Christian with me. Christian's mother and I had joint custody, and he stayed with me throughout the summer.

He's a good kid who loves his daddy to pieces, and he's smart but not smart enough to be left alone at eight years old. I couldn't get a sitter for that evening, so he accompanied me to the Clyburn Inn where the meeting was to be held. After I walked into the front lobby area, I immediately spotted a gentleman on the sofa having a conversation with another person. My attention was focused on him, and I assumed that he was Clyburn Gray simply by the way he spoke. He spoke with sort of a high-pitched voice but none that I could readily identify from this part of the region. He finished up his conversation and then turned his total attention to me and my son. "Detective Monroe?"

Being this man I've never seen who recognized me by my name, it was easy to confirm my assumption that he was Mr. Gray. He greeted me with a very warm smile and a firm, manly handshake and told me that it was a pleasure to finally meet me. He said he heard a lot of things about me. I assumed it was good when I saw him smiling as he said it. Not only did this rich black man acknowledge me, but he also acknowledged my son Christian. He politely spoke with him, shook his hand, and had brief small talk with him as I listened and admired his candor. When he spoke to my son in that fashion, I knew then that he was a compassionate man who could appreciate family values. Even though I didn't have the ideal family complete with a wife and children under the same roof, I had my son who was my responsibility. Mr. Gray recognized that and respected it, which in turn made me respect him even more. The three of us sat in the lobby with the desk clerk sitting behind the checkout counter just a few feet away. The conversation remained on the lighter side while we sat in the lobby but turned to a much more serious and sincere conversation after he asked me to accompany him to the dining area. It was time for business. I instructed Christian to remain in the lobby and watch television as I followed Mr. Gray into the quiet dining area where we sat alone.

We sat, and he talked candidly about his granddaughter Sallie whose murder was still unresolved. He opened the conversation by telling me about himself and the family he never knew. He told me with pride that the Hatcher family is his family. Adele is his daughter, and her children are and were his grandchildren. Gray, as everyone called him, had no problem expressing the love he had for his family, regardless of who they were or where they came from. He told me that he first learned of his family from a friend who resided in Lawrence County. Gray never told me who the friend was, and I really didn't care to know, but whoever it was, I'm sure he owes him a great deal of gratitude. Gray told me he and his friend from Lawrence would call each other from time to time, and it was a friend he trusted. He said one day the friend called him with some news he thought was ludicrous and absurd. The friend informed Gray that he believed Gray had family ties in Lawrence. In fact, the friend also told him that he thought it was his daughter who lived in Lawrence, and that it was his granddaughter that was murdered. This conversation was interesting to me to say the least. I was talking directly to Gray, the man responsible for everything that had taken place with the Hatchers and the establishment I sat in. We were talking like we knew each other in an unsolicited, open conversation. He told me it was his first time ever hearing anything of this magnitude, but he trusted his friend to get the truth and tell him the truth. He told his friend to fish around quietly and let him know when he finds the truth about the Hatchers. He told me he didn't know what to think, but that the information had to be a mistake. He said he had a few women in his younger years, but none in the south that bore any kids by him. But he wanted to be sure because if there was a slight chance that he had a daughter, he wanted to know her. The friend assured Gray that he would not ever speak of it again unless he confirmed the information to be true.

It was several weeks later that Gray said he received another call from the friend from Lawrence. This call would be a turning point in Gray's otherwise-busy life. The information was confirmed. Gray had fathered a child by the name of Adele, and he was the grandfather to four beautiful girls. I began to see Mr. Gray smile as he spoke about his daughter and her children, and I began to see his eyes tearing as well as did mine. That moment was one that I will never forget. To see a man of his caliber have some sense of moral character, humbleness, and speak with such grace really moved me. He became to me more than a man with money, but a man of dignity. I wondered if he took the time to tell his story to others like he did me, or if we just connected with each other. I don't know the answer, but it felt like it was just he and I, and I knew then that I would never expose his story or compromise his trust that he had in me. Gray's friend didn't hold back anything, and he definitely did his homework. Gray was told about his daughter, the children, and even about Adele's deadbeat husband. Gray said he couldn't believe how poor his family was. It made him sick inside to know he had a family who had been suffering all this time, and he knew nothing about them. "When I met Adele for the first time, Monroe, tears came into my eyes, and I couldn't stop crying. I've got money, Monroe, but what good is money if you can't do anything good with it? I bought this establishment for my family and put them in charge of it, and if they do well with it, I will be happy." I could see the level of sincerity as we continued to talk. I knew this was no joke, and it was a monumental moment for him and not one of his many projects, but a moment he wasn't prepared for but welcomed with open arms. Gray said he had to do something, anything to help during their tragic time. He had the means, and he was determined to bond his family and hopefully bring a positive change to their lives.

Gray then turned up the heat of the conversation even more when he began to focus on the subject at hand, which was the death of his granddaughter. He told me he heard about the killing and how it happened and asked me if there were any leads on the son of a bitch who did this horrible thing to his granddaughter. I hesitated as I usually do to allow myself time to carefully choose the words projected from my mouth. I knew if I said the wrong thing at the wrong time, it could turn our conversation into an unpleasant one. "Well," I said, followed by a few twitches of the mouth and a couple of noises with my tongue and teeth, which is my trademark of stall time until I am ready to answer. I finally began to answer his question and informed him that the case was still wide open and currently still under investigation. I told him we were still following up on leads and all relevant information as we received it. Even though that was true, a feeling of despair came over me because I knew we (the police department) were not doing enough. I felt he also knew the police department wasn't doing enough. However, being as tactful as he was, he wouldn't dare say anything negative about the PD or its representatives. So not only was I carefully choosing my words, he was carefully choosing his as well. At no time did Gray ever mention the fact that he was the one who put up the $25,000 reward in Sallie's case. How absolutely modest. I just knew at the beginning of our meeting, I would probably hear a lot of vain and self-accomplished remarks, but not one so far. The only time he did mention anything about himself was near the beginning of the conversation when he was laying out the premise of his presence in Lawrence, which was sort of essential to my understanding him.

Gray told me he would do whatever was necessary to solve Sallie Hatcher's murder. "Anything," he emphasized. I didn't quite understand where he was going with our conversation, but I continued to listen with my ever so inquisitive ears. I suppose he wanted me to dig further and find answers, and he assured me no price was too much to find his granddaughter's killer.

I knew there was nothing more I could have done, and no amount of money could solve Sallie Hatcher's case. Although I had an idea what his implications and preconceived notions were, I thought about my loyalty to the police department as well as my own morals and ethics, and we quickly ended all talks of money. I did assure him we would continue to work diligently on the case until someone was apprehended. Gray continued talking and asked me if I would mind if he hired a private investigator to work on the case. I quickly told him that the decision was not mine to make, but I would be open to any and all relevant information that could be obtained by the PI. Shortly after my responses, our conversation began to conclude, and I could see the interest diminish. Gray asked me to call him if I needed anything and pleaded with me to stay in touch with him as the case developed. I agreed. We shook hands, and I walked back into the lobby area where I got my son who had been most patient, and we left. I left feeling like Gray had just put me on the spot, and he was depending on me. I really wanted the monkey off my back, but what was I supposed to do or say? As always, I wanted to do a good job and bring this case to a close, so again I carried the weight of this case on my shoulders for me, for the police department, for the community, for Gray, for the family, and for Sallie.

CHAPTER 21

End of an Era

Even though we continued to sporadically examine the case, nothing ever really changed in the investigation. No new information, no new sources, and nowhere to go. Lieutenant Poesley seemed to continue with a lack of interest in the case, but I would have to think I was wrong in my assumptions. He had to be just as frustrated as we were, but he was never one to display his emotions openly. He tried to act like nothing bothered him. Anyone in their right mind would have been touched by this case, especially those who lived here and was raised here, and Lieutenant Poesley was no exception. Not long after I met Gray, the lieutenant announced that he would be running for sheriff in the year 2002 and would leave the police department whether he won the election or not. One thing I knew about the lieutenant was that he was an honest man, and if he told anyone he was going to do something, he kept his word. He did run for sheriff but lost the election by a landslide to another hometown hero. Not long after his devastating loss in the election, the lieutenant retired.

I really hated to see the lieutenant leave the department as I grew increasingly fond of him and sort of looked at him as a father figure I never had. I think we had a mutual respect, and I think his compassion and feelings for me mirrored mine, although we never spoke of it. We did not always agree, and we bumped heads on more than a few occasions because of our differences of opinions and methods on getting the job done. But he brought laughter and character to a place that would otherwise be a dull and humdrum place. I looked forward to stopping by his office in the morning and sharing a laugh with him. He was always in good spirit and would not only give me a laugh in the morning, but periodically throughout the day. I don't even think he knew when he was being funny; it just came naturally. We all knew his time was up, and he made the right decision by retiring. And as I suspected, the office ambiance changed, and the constant laughter and light-affair conversations diminished.

Ironically, his retirement celebration was given at the Clyburn Inn banquet room, which was the very essence of Sallie Hatcher's memory. I could not seem to forget that this motel existed because of Sallie Hatcher, but yet here we were celebrating in her house as her murder went unsolved. To some people, we were patronizing an African American business, but to a few others, it was a slap in the face. Even I didn't think about how the ceremony would be perceived until my arrival there, and I saw Sallie Hatcher's mother. Mrs. Hatcher never said anything harsh to anyone that night, and she and her staff displayed the utmost professionalism throughout the entire affair. The entrées were delicious and cooked to perfection. The ceremony lasted about two hours as Lieutenant Poesley's friends, family, and coworkers toasted for him.

Finally, it was Lieutenant Poesley's turn at the podium, and he spoke with great conviction and sincerity as he spoke of his profession and love. The lieutenant was a Baptist minister, so public speaking came easy to him. He told the audience he wanted to share one of his most memorable moments with us, which was a moment he said he would never forget, a moment that kept him awake at night, a moment that "ate at me." The room became very quiet, and everybody in the room stood still and became most attentive. As I sat in my seat, I looked around the room and wondered if there were other people thinking and feeling what I was feeling at that time. Given the place we were celebrating, the people who were hosting the celebration and the magnitude of such a baffling case, I just knew that Sallie Hatcher would be at the top of his list. I wanted Sallie Hatcher's name to ring out in that banquet hall, and I strongly wanted the lieutenant to exalt her name on behalf of the police department, so everyone would know we care.

He began telling how a young lady's child was kidnapped and how good it felt to be able to return the child to her mother. He told us how devastating the case was and how much time he spent trying to bring the case to a close. Soon after he began to tell his account of the case, I drifted off, feeling somewhat disappointed in the story he spoke of. Even though I'm sure it was a heart-wrenching event to see a mother lose a child, the abduction took place about twenty years ago. Sallie was killed just two years ago! She too was taken from her mother and left two kids behind. But if that was the moment he will never forget, I guess I have to accept his honesty. Maybe I was the only one with that empty feeling of sadness for Sallie Hatcher. I seemed to have lost most of the content of the lieutenant's story, but I do remember him ending his story by telling us he will never forget the look on the mother's face when he returned her child to her and how good it made him feel. An investigator's greatest satisfaction comes when a case is solved, and maybe, just maybe because Sallie Hatcher's case was unsolved was the reason why it wasn't the lieutenant's most memorable moment. I just don't know.

I miss the lieutenant dearly since his departure. He often brought an unexpected joy and laughter to the division that had not yet been surpassed by anyone, and I don't think it ever will. Chief Mallory tried to connect with us from time to time, but he surely was not a natural. He struggled with long, drawn-out jokes that never really made anyone laugh, and by the time he reached the punch line, the joke had lost its effect altogether. We would chuckle a bit anyway to make him feel better, and besides that, he was our boss, and it was almost like we were compelled to show some positive emotion. The lieutenant sort of disappeared after his retirement and put most of his time into pastoring a neighboring church in Rockingham, North Carolina. When I saw him, it was usually somewhere in the neighborhood or during my visits to his home. It was truly an end of an era. The Lieutenant was in his late sixties when he retired and eventually passed away in 2017.

The chief never gained his momentum back for the job, but he stayed around for reasons I don't know. I've heard officers stick around beyond their retirement years because of a sense of loneliness, and/or financial hardships became more of a burden when the retiree hasn't prepared for departure. I don't know why Mallory chose to stay; maybe it was just to keep his mind occupied to avoid any thought of his son's tragedy. He and Poesley were the department's icons who sometimes acted more like brothers than coworkers. I never thought I would see the day when one would leave the department without the other, but obviously, that was only my thought and not theirs.

Two years had just about passed us by, and we welcomed the new year of 2003, which was just about the anniversary of Sallie's death. The memory of her death only seemed to exist to those who occasionally saw her picture posted on the walls of convenience stores or plastered to the glass at the front desk of the police department. There was no more talk or wonder about what happened to her, and Lawrence seemed to return to its normal dormant existence. Petty crime continued, and people roamed the streets again as if they forgot there was still a killer on the loose. Even my thoughts and aggressions were subdued somewhat, and my eagerness to catch the killer diminished and eroded in hopes that Sallie's death was a one-time deal, and we would never have to experience that kind of ordeal again. As eager as I once was to catch the killer, I was satisfied merely with the fact that it wouldn't happen again, at least in our city.

CHAPTER 22

The Next Devastation

My hopes and dreams were totally shattered the morning of January 24, 2003. Friday was a normal day despite the snow that was still on the ground. It was chilly at about forty degrees. The sun was out, and it was the last day of my workweek. I had a mound of paperwork that I had pummeled through and conquered throughout the week, and I was ready to sit back and relax over the weekend with my son. I had talked to Christian on the phone and assured him that Daddy would pick him up promptly at 5:30 PM. I looked forward to our father-son time because his mother and I divorced several years earlier. We lived in different cities, and I didn't get as much time with him as I would have liked to. Therefore, I made the little time shared between us as quality time. I was careful not to bring my work home, and whatever cases I had opened during the week, I would normally put them on hold until my next business day, which was after my son had gone back to his mother. Most of the time it worked, but on this day, it did not.

I heard a call go out over the police radio. The telecommunicator instructed a squad car to check a residence on Tara Drive in reference to an open door found by school officials. We got calls like that all the time, so I didn't give it a second thought. Either someone mistakenly left their door open, or it was just another break-in, I thought. As I was admiring the beautiful snow-covered trees and rooftops from the driver's seat of my police cruiser, a second call came over the radio about fifteen minutes later from Lieutenant Matt Godwin who requested Detective Sardoms to meet him at a house located at 1200 Tara Drive. Matt's voice had a different tone as he spoke over the radio. It was a sound of concern and somewhat like a voice of distress that hardly anyone would recognize. He tried to speak calmly, but I could tell something just wasn't right. Moments later, I heard Detective Sardoms call for Detective Woodland to respond to the house. I knew then that it was something serious, but I was still hoping it was nothing of major concern, but maybe, just maybe, it wasn't serious enough to cancel my weekend with Christian.

I still had no idea what the call was about, but after hearing the calls for assistance, I knew I had to go see or go to assist. I made a U-turn in the roadway and headed in their direction, still hoping everything was okay. I was about a half mile from the residence in question and anxiously waited for someone to cancel my procession as they sometimes do if the situation could quickly be resolved. I continued to drive toward Tara Drive without any radio interruption and finally arrived at a house located only yards from Sallie's old apartment.

The house was a gray wood-framed house with a front door that led into a living room and a left side door that led into a kitchen from the vacant carport. The house looked pretty ordinary other than the side door being ajar. It looked like a break-in, and I was put at ease at the point where I saw the open door. Surely, that was all it could have been since there was a house located right next to it and apartments on the opposite side of the street. But I was bewildered why all the attention, and did this simple case of burglary really require two detectives and a lieutenant?

Detective Sardoms met us outside at the side entrance of the house with a grim look. Before he said anything, I knew something terrible was about to come out of his mouth. His face was a bit flushed as officers and neighbors gathered outside in the roadway. He began to tell us what he had witnessed inside the house. Little did I know that the next words that came from his mouth would rock this town again as well as myself for a second time. Detective Sardoms told us that Loretta Miles Brodus was supposed to report for work that morning at North Lawrence School; however, she had not shown up by eleven o'clock, which prompted school officials to check on her. Officials said it was unlike Loretta to be late or miss work, so they sent a couple of counselors to her house to check and see what the problem was.

The counselors saw the side door open, went a few feet inside, and saw a large trail of blood that led endlessly into another room. The counselors went no further for fear of the unknown and quickly retreated outside. They contacted the school and called 911. Detective Sardoms told us when he arrived and got the information from the counselors. He went in to investigate along with another officer. He told us about the massive blood trail that led all the way from the kitchen to Loretta's bedroom. He told us that along the blood trail were a set of teeth lying on the floor that had apparently been kicked out of Loretta's mouth. "It's bad, oh my god, it's bad," Clyde repeated as he spoke.

The trail led to Loretta's bedroom where her lifeless body lay stretched across her bed and partially nude as her hands and feet were bound together and hog-tied to the bedpost. Sardoms was devastated as he nervously described the condition of Loretta's lifeless body. He told us whoever committed this murder possibly raped her as well because of the lack of clothes on her body and the way she was posed and positioned on her bed.

A feeling of disbelief came over me as well as a feeling of despair and anger all over again. I immediately thought of Sallie Hatcher and didn't want to believe the nightmare was happening all over again. The son of a bitch just killed another defenseless black woman and insulted the police department for a second time. What the hell did we have living among us in our quaint small town? This wasn't the normal boyfriend-girlfriend or drug-related killing or any other killing that could have been explained. This was a killing done by an unconscientious monster. A monster who didn't really have a reason for killing, but maybe just for the joy of it, and yet we had no clue on who killed either victim. How many more girls would be killed before we caught this monster? All these thoughts circled around and around in my mind as we stood there talking with Sardoms. After he told us what he saw, I somewhat disconnected and got into my own world of anger all over again, but my disconnection didn't last long because there was work to be done.

We normally rotated cases among the detectives depending on everyone's caseload. Sardoms had the Hatcher homicide, and I inherited the case of Loretta Miles Brodus.

CHAPTER 23

A Mirrored Scene

After the decision was finalized for me to take the case, Sardoms led me into the house. He showed me what looked like a gruesome and eerie crime scene that one could only imagine or see in a movie. The more I witnessed, the angrier I became. We entered through the left side door, which was located under the open-air carport, which also served as a temporary command post where officers gathered to exchange information among ourselves without being overheard. Only those who needed to know were allowed on the property and under the carport. Many neighbors and other people gathered outside the boundary line to catch a glimpse of anything they could see or hear. They had to know in their minds that something was dreadfully wrong. Officers had surrounded the house with yellow crime-scene tape, didn't allow anyone to go beyond that point, and whispered only among themselves. We were all very careful not to discuss anything with anyone outside our circle about the scene or about what we saw. We did not even discuss the case with our fellow officers because we had to maintain a certain level of control and integrity throughout the case. We knew our officers wouldn't intentionally share privileged information, but even I am guilty of pillow talk.

As we entered through the vestibule from the carport, I saw blood…lots of blood. As I looked around, I saw what appeared to be shoestrings tied to different fixed objects within the kitchen. One string was tied to a door handle while the other was tied to the handle of a cabinet. It looked as if some type of sadistic ritual had taken place. From the amount of blood, it was easy to tell a struggle had taken place in that same area, and the victim offered strong resistance and apparently fought for her life. The large splatters of blood gave me an eerie feeling of confusion of what I could expect. None of us were used to homicides of such a bizarre nature. The few homicides we did have in our city were usually quick, unplanned, and domestic related, which made it easy for us to track a suspect with the exception of Sallie Hatcher's. We maintained a high arrest and conviction rate, and we were proud of that fact, until Sallie, but hopefully, we would redeem ourselves by finding Loretta Brodus's killer.

As we entered the kitchen, the large pool of blood turned into a trail that led throughout the kitchen and through the dining room. As we continued to walk, I noticed dinner had been cooked, and a full pot of spaghetti was on the stove undisturbed with the stove turned off. As I tried to decipher this puzzle and quickly piece it together, I assumed Loretta was caught off guard and disturbed by something or someone, which was the reason for the uneaten spaghetti. It could have been a noise outside or an acquaintance knocking at her door. As we continued to walk straight out of the kitchen area and into a quaint adjoining dining area, it was obvious she had set a place for only her to eat at the rectangular-shaped glass table, but the plate was clean. There was only one plate on the table, which was indicative she was home alone. The only other items on the table was her mail, which consisted of some unpaid and delinquent bills. Her prescription glasses lay amid all the papers she had scattered about. Even though the blood trail traveled through the dining room, there were no other signs of struggle thus far as the trail led us into the living room. I could only guess that Loretta had been severely beaten, stabbed, or shot at this point, and dragged about the house as she was probably begging desperately for her life.

The trail of coagulated blood led us to the left of the dining area and into the living room where I thought I would finally see Loretta's body, but instead of seeing Loretta, I saw where the most serious altercation took place. This was indeed where Loretta fought for her life and breathed her last breath. A fight and struggle ensued in the living room where the couch had been overturned, and other household items were knocked to the floor and broken. One of the most unusual broken items we found that had apparently fell onto the floor at one time was a ceramic religious figurine of the Last Supper. The position of the figurine was most disturbing and puzzling. Although the couch had been knocked over during the struggle, the figurine of the Last Supper was placed on top of the turned-over couch. It appeared to be carefully placed as it sat at the center of the couch. The head of Jesus Christ was decapitated while all the other disciples were deliberately left intact. What did this all mean? Probably only the killer would know for sure. If I were to surmise my own opinion, I believe the killer had some level of moral character and maybe a decent upbringing by a decent family. Since the killer was conscious enough to realize he was the one who knocked Christ and his disciples to the floor, his moral character, however small, compelled him to at least pick up the figurine and neatly place it on the couch. Several hypotheses came to mind. Either he broke off the head of Christ because he didn't want Christ to see the devastation he caused to an innocent being, or he had no respect for Christ at all and broke his head off as it made him feel more superior to Christ. Or the head could have broken off during the fall and the killer just didn't bother to pick it up, but we never found the head of Christ. Either way, this was not a normal person and not a normal crime scene. It became even more bizarre as we continued our observation.

Another disturbing moment came as I continued to stand in the living room, looking for any clues I could find. What I found was an upper plate of false teeth lying on the floor soaked and engorged with blood just as Clyde described. Though Clyde had already warned us what we would see, it was something that I could have never imagined. This case was beginning to be another one of Lawrence's most horrific encounters since Sallie. When I saw the dislodged plate of teeth drenched in blood, I had to brace myself on what was to come. I could sense death all around me. I visualized this helpless woman dying at the hands of a monster as he kicked and stabbed her repeatedly, but I needed to see the body. I needed to see it to understand it, to analyze it, and to investigate it.

After taking a brief overview of the living room, we continued to follow the blood trail. The trail took a left turn as we followed it through the hallway. The hallway was only about fifteen feet long from the beginning to the end and about five feet wide, but it seemed like it took me forever to get to the end of that hall because I knew the end of the hall was the inevitable.

As we walked down the hallway toward Loretta's bedroom, the blood became less. I assumed she had lost most of her blood in the kitchen and living room where she fought fiercely and fearlessly to survive. The bedroom had a few things lying about, but nothing terribly out of the ordinary with the exception of Loretta's half-naked body strewn across the bed as if she was a rag doll. Her feet had been bound together as were her hands, with clear indications of deep ligature marks and lacerations located on her ankles and wrists. Her legs were separated and spread apart as wide as they could possibly spread, as her left leg dangled off the side of the bed.

It was apparent to me that some sick excuse for a human being had bludgeoned her to death before he dragged her into the bedroom where he possibly raped her on her own bed. The blood from her head soaked the light-colored sheets, and her eyes gazed into nowhere as she lay face up in her own blood. The moment I saw her was the moment I knew this was committed by some sick and erotic sexual deviant whom she probably knew. The average murderer, if such a person existed, would not have taken the time to kill a woman in this calculated fashion. From beginning to the end of this murder rampage, it probably took about three hours or more to accomplish such preciseness and detail as well as deal with the physical confrontation. This was no ordinary homicide. The murder suspect clearly wanted to humiliate Loretta for some unknown reason. That reason is what we had to figure out.

I took a deep breath, looked at Loretta's once-beautiful and unblemished body, and cried internally for her, her family, the Hatcher family, and all other defenseless women who could possibly become victims. I even cried for myself because I felt like a failure for not finding Sallie's killer. Maybe, just maybe, if her killer would have been found and arrested, maybe Loretta would still be alive. I needed strength, and I desperately needed renewal and guidance just as we all did in order to bring about new and fresh ideas. Within that same moment of internal combustion, I prayed to God that this barbarian would not kill another woman in our city. I prayed for strength, endurance, and perseverance in this case because I knew if the killer wasn't caught, he would surely kill again. After I fought the demons within myself and asked for guidance, I quickly became anew. I became determined, regenerated, and reinvigorated to turn our town upside down and go beyond the call of duty to get the bastard responsible for the deaths of these innocent women.

I gave everyone orders not to touch anything and not to let anyone on to the crime scene. Although Clyde had already given the order, I wanted to make sure I was heard, and I wanted everyone to know I meant business. I directed the crime-scene technician, Victor Torres, to keep all nonofficial persons away and as far from the scene as possible. Even most of our law enforcement officials were denied access to the scene for fear of contamination. I instructed several uniformed officers to stand at different strategic points to make sure we had a 360-degree view of the house and to make sure we had full control of anyone coming in or going out of the scene. I then placed a call to the police department to request additional personnel to help with the investigation. I knew it was only a matter of time that a massive crowd of neighbors and family would gather, and we would definitely need the additional help. All personnel were instructed to get a pen and paper and record any and all relevant information as well as anyone they see around the crime scene. Most of the officers were inquisitive by nature, and we usually share information with each other, but on this occasion, we did not. This crime scene was on a need-to-know basis, and nobody needed to know except those of us investigating the tragedy. We briefed them as best we could without insulting anyone by giving them lackluster information. It was crucial that we got everything right the first time on this one.

I felt like everyone in the neighborhood was looking at us and watching our every move, but they were most likely only interested in what happened to Loretta. I felt like they all already knew Loretta was dead but was anxiously waiting to hear it from one of us or from whoever could eavesdrop. Security was tight that day because another slipup could very well cost us another life. I think we all had the same thoughts in mind, and we all wanted to catch this heinous killer before he was able to kill again.

As I constantly talked with the other detectives, I could see the frustration in their eyes and in their conversation. It was almost like we were sitting on the edge of our seats at a movie theater and wondering what the hell was going to happen next. Even though I gave assignments and was conscious of what I was doing, I came to a point where I felt completely mute. Officers were steadily talking to me, but I blocked out and filtered through a lot of their conversation until something of importance captured my attention. Their conversations were like a blur to me as I listened to them and gathered my thoughts simultaneously. It was September 11, 2001, when the World Trade Center was bombed. I recall media and other people adamantly questioning why former president George W. Bush did nothing and was nonresponsive for seven minutes in front of a kindergarten class on that notorious day. Even though I formed my own opinion about Bush's action or lack thereof, finding Loretta's body made it all clear to me and confirmed my thoughts because I found myself in the same transfixed condition. I stood there for several minutes absorbing and deciphering information as well as figuring out a plan on how to deal with this case. Time was of the essence, and I didn't need to waste any of it purposely running around and accomplishing nothing. Questions came to mind like, Who should I call? Who will be doing what? Who were Loretta's associates? What was the motive behind her death, and who did it? There were so many things to be done, and I was the quarterback. So yes, I did absolutely nothing for several minutes but thought of what needed to be done.

Before I began to get deeply involved, I had to remember I was a father, and I had to somehow call my son and delicately break the news to him that I would not be able to get him for the weekend and that Daddy had to catch a killer. I called him and apologized for not being able to pick him up as planned. I knew and felt his disappointment, but Christian knew the perils of my job, and as young as he was, he understood and said, "I'll see ya next week, Dad." His understanding gave me great relief because it relieved me of my sorrow for him, and it cleared my mind from personal interferences.

After snapping back to the moment at hand, I began barking out even more orders and replayed the voices of several people as they questioned me and spoke to me in a quest for answers. Most of the bystanders would ask me questions like "Is she dead?" "Who found her?" "What happened?" "Did you call her family?" etc. Officers were constantly asking me what to do, What happened in there? You want me to get everybody's name? They knew they asked me questions I wasn't at liberty to answer, but they continuously tried anyway in hopes of getting some insight of what happened. One officer, our juvenile officer Daryl Wilcox, even told me that somebody named Toby Singleton was walking around asking about the woman who was stabbed. Wilcox asked me if I wanted him to get his name because he thought it was strange since nobody mentioned anything about stabbing. I think I snapped at him for asking me such a question only because he knew the answer. I simply responded, "Yes, get his name and address."

The house was secure, the scene was secure, and officers were briefed and given assignments. Reporting persons, associates, and coworkers of Loretta's had been separated and were standing by to be interviewed. My next step was to contact the North Carolina State Bureau of Investigation to request assistance from their mobile crime lab. It was routine for us to contact the SBI crime lab for any major or bizarre crime such as this one because we did not have the proper resources available, and we could not expedite the necessary inquiries on items like bank records, credit cards, telephone records, etc. Nor did we have personnel to sufficiently process the crime scene. We had a crime-scene investigator, but he had not been with us long enough to sufficiently deal with a case of this magnitude. I called special agent-in-charge Janice Suttles via cell phone, briefed her of the circumstances, and requested the assistance of the mobile crime lab. Janie, as we call her, was most helpful, even though she was out of town; she contacted and requested several agents to assist in the case to include special agent Melania Jeffrey, who was in charge of the crime lab. All the agents met with us in front of Loretta's house in less than an hour after Janie and I spoke. I knew it was going to be an all-day affair based on what I had seen. Even though the house had signs of struggle, the house was still somewhat neat in my opinion. It was a little too neat for someone to have struggled and fought with Loretta as she was no small lady. There was really no telling how long it would take to process the house, so we all prepared for an all-nighter.

This marks the first time our crime-scene technician had been exposed to this kind of case, one that had to be handled so delicately. The work would be tedious, time consuming, and exhausting for the crime-scene techs, but Bobby Woodland was about to learn some invaluable lessons that day. He armed himself with a blue protective suit, gloves, booties, and a facial mask as he prepared to get down and dirty right alongside Melania. She would probably teach him more about a crime scene in two days than most techs would learn in six months. I was proud of him for being able to face the pressure and being able to take a back seat to the experienced professional. He stayed with Melania's every step and followed her commands as she gave them.

On the following day, sometime in the late evening, they called us to the scene and gave us a report that brought gloom to our hopes and wishes. They told us they were unable to find any evidence in the house despite the intense search. Despite the many hours they put in processing, they found no real evidence to link us to the killer. I could see the disappointment and frustration on their faces as they described to us the methods they used to process. Surely, I thought some form of evidence had to be found. Surely, after such a brutal killing of this nature, the killer had to leave some evidence behind, and yet we were told nothing was found.

This was extremely scary because not only did we have a monster on the loose and in our midst, it appeared the killer was smart and had all the makings of a serial killer. This was something I've read about and seen on television, but I never imagined that I would be part of such real-life story. All indicators revealed that of a serial killer; Loretta was killed in the same fashion as her neighbor Sallie. She was killed in the same neighborhood and just across the street from Sallie. The time of death was within close proximity of each other;

both females were school administrators, both females were African American, attractive with long black hair. Both females apparently knew their killer, both were raped, both bodies were posed for display, and both were hog-tied by their wrists and ankles with what looked like normal shoestring. Both were possibly sodomized, and both were fatally and repeatedly beaten and stabbed by their attacker. One odd and unidentifiable characteristic of both crime scenes was a sandy, grainy substance found on both victim's floors. The substance had the feel and texture of common table salt, but we could not readily identify it. We simply collected samples of the substance for testing later.

I was somewhat relieved when Melania and Bob told us they were not finished with the crime scene but simply needed a break, and they were going back in for more. She told us she did everything she could think of in search of evidence but just was not able to find the slightest piece of evidence. But she was yet to use the chemical agent called luminol, which is a chemical compound that reacts with human blood that illuminates and glows to a bright bluish color when mixed with certain other reactive agents. It is a product often used by law enforcement to detect the presence of blood when traces of blood cannot be seen with the naked eye. I think we all had our fingers crossed this time, hoping they would find something to help us solve the case. This case brought us together in many ways and at a later time took us further apart from each other. Even though we were glad to see the crime-scene techs go back in the house, we didn't get our hopes up because we didn't want to face another disappointment. All the investigators left the scene once more and allowed the crime-scene techs to continue their business with explicit directions to call us if and soon as they found something or at their conclusion.

Hours later, about seven o'clock, we got the call from Bob letting us know they were finished. I tried to decipher whether Bob had any excitement in his voice, but I couldn't tell. I wanted an answer before we arrived back at the scene, but Bob didn't give me any indication whatsoever, which wasn't a good sign in my mind. We arrived to find Bob and Melania in front of the house at their vehicles, taking off their protective garb and packing up their tools as if it was all over.

They stopped what they were doing and told us how unbelievably clean the crime scene was, and they searched the house from top to bottom but wasn't able to recover any evidence other than a shoe impression that was found in the dining room area.

    The impression looked like a boot, maybe a Timberland style, but she couldn't be sure of the brand. She said they would have never seen the print if it were not for the luminol. However, that one shoe impression was the only one they could find in the house. How amazing is that after all the time spent in the house while killing Loretta, posing her body and sodomizing her, the killer had time to literally clean up after himself as it so appeared. Melania told us that instead of trying to extract the impression by conventional methods, she was going to remove part of the floor containing the shoeprint. She said it would be the best way to preserve it in an undisturbed state until she could have it examined at the state crime lab in Raleigh. Even this piece of evidence was not a groundbreaker because even if the shoe was identified, we still had nobody to connect the shoe with. I was sure that whatever the boot type, there were probably thousands more made just like it. I pretty much discounted the impression and continued to think of other ways to tackle this case. The investigation still seemed bleak to me, and I still had no answers. But then again, something was better than nothing. We thanked Melania for helping us, and we were sure in our minds that she did the best she could, and if there was anything else in that house, she would have found it. Melania was very knowledgeable, eager, and ready to get the job done, and she enjoyed her work as well as the results she achieved from it. We had all the confidence in the world in her, and we knew there was nothing more we could do with the house. The house was shut down and released to Loretta's family.

CHAPTER 24

Alternatives

As the weeks went by and we waited for lab results, we met regularly with all our investigators and investigators from the state bureau. At the beginning of our series of meetings, the entire division would come together to discuss the case. Those meetings consisted of quite a few of us but dwindled down in attendance as time passed. It was great at the beginning because we got a chance to examine the evidence and our thoughts and ideas and exchanged ideologies of fellow law enforcement personnel with a vast array of experience and expertise. I knew and accepted that I could not do it alone, and I needed the aid of my counterparts. Most of the meetings at the beginning consisted of myself; narcotics detectives Gene Murcey, Kevon Stricklen, Clyde Sardoms, Audrey Woodland; crime-scene investigator Bobby Woodland, juvenile investigator Daryl Wilcox; and SBI Agent Sullivan. Together, we started examining the case from the beginning and covering any ground that needed to be more thoroughly examined. No stone was to go uncovered, and we were allowed to discuss in detail whatever was on our minds. The meetings were especially difficult though because we had to compare two homicides, and we had to compare and analyze evidence or lack thereof from two years prior.

After days of analyzing and comparing notes, we eventually came up with a target list of suspects, which consisted of some of the same suspects from Sallie's case.

Among those suspects were Jaston Setler, Sallie's part-time lover who we never completely ruled out as a suspect; Ricardo Delsado, Sallie's ex-lover as well as her daughter's father who was also a prime suspect in Sallie's case; Charlie Pounds, a convicted murderer from New York who lived just yards from Loretta. Sallie's mail carrier Ted was another suspect who we subsequently found out raped a woman in the same apartment complex where Sallie lived. Also on the list was Roberto Puff Loveton, Toby Singleton, Larry "Pop" Wilcox, and Donald Mathews who were all outside and next door to Loretta's house on the night of her murder. Earl James McLaurin, Ricardo Hobson, and Timothy Smith were more people of interest and acquaintances of Sallie's. Jeff Brodus, Loretta's estranged husband, quickly became the primary suspect. Jeff Brodus had documents and official police records of arrest while living in New York. He was accused and found guilty of abuse after he severely beat his girlfriend. There was also a local city commissioner who we subsequently found out he was also sharing Sallie's company. John Williams was an older gentleman who had been in politics for quite some time. He was married and somewhat respected in the community. We definitely didn't want to ruin his reputation or let him know he was also a suspect. We had to be very discreet because he was actually one of the people who controlled our salaries and other department necessities. There came an occasion where one of our detectives were at a social function with Williams. The detective quickly swiped the empty drinking glass after, Williams placed it on the table. His DNA was to be submitted just like everyone else.

The list of suspects would bring us a lot of work trying to incorporate or eliminate each suspect. But we surely thought that out of all the listed suspects, the killer was one of them. What we did know in our minds is that whoever killed Sallie also killed Loretta. The two crimes were definitely connected, and it was obvious the killer was no stranger to either victim.

Our many legal pads became full of information. We had diagrams of the victim's houses, diagrams of the victim's bodies, and diagrams of the crime locations from both a land and aerial view plastered around the room. Anyone who joined us at any time during our meeting would surely be confused by the massive amount of information clustered about the room. Because there was such an abundant amount of crucial information shared and exchanged, Detective Woodland demanded we be present at every meeting so we would not miss anything of vital importance. For days, we went over and over the information until nothing new came out of it. The meetings then became less often as time continued, and we still could not narrow down a suspect. However, Jeff Brodus was still a prime suspect because of his past relationship in New York and his connection with Loretta.

Detective Woodland and Special Agent Sullivan's opinion about Brodus being the killer was so strong, they compiled a list of incriminating evidence against him. They gave him a motive; they provided him with the opportunity to kill Loretta even though he had logged in hours with his trucking company around the time Loretta was killed. They also described his state of mind since he could not be with Loretta.

The chief knew we were getting frustrated, and he began to be targeted for ridicule by us as well as by the community. Public opinions and scrutiny started shifting in his direction as the detectives became less of a focal point. People started asking what he was doing about the case and complained of not seeing him in the community or consoling or showing any compassion toward either of the families.

About a month after our meetings began, Chief Mallory called a meeting with us. I thought either he was going to chastise us for not being able to close either case, or he simply wanted to know our progress as he sometimes did. Well, it turned out that he didn't want to do either. He told us a profiler from the Federal Bureau of Investigation would be meeting with us the following week. He gave us a short biography of the profiler and told us the agent would be traveling to Lawrence from Quantico, Virginia.

That was good news to my ears because obviously these cases were out of my league, so I thought, and I had high hopes the FBI would help us get to the bottom of our crimes.

The following week, we indeed met with the profiler who was dressed in a nice suit and obviously very knowledgeable about his discipline. I was all ears and most attentive as he introduced himself to us. We were all present with the exception of the chief, who I thought should have been present to listen just for mere practical purposes or to get some answers he did not have. After giving us his background, the profiler began to lightly talk about our cases but in no specific detail. As he continued to talk and give us his thoughts, I became somewhat despondent as he spoke about things that were sort of obvious to me as it should have been to the other trained investigators in the room. He gave us an average age range of people who normally commit crimes of this nature. He told us the person responsible for both deaths was most likely somebody from the community or not far from the community, and he told us the killer most likely had some feeling of abnormal gratification from sex as he killed his prey. I continued to listen objectively and waited for him to tell me something I didn't already know. I was waiting for him to take the rein from us and guide us to the right path. I wanted him to assure us that there were high solvability factors, and the case would most likely be solved, but instead, I got nothing but an invitation to go to Quantico and sit down with other profilers of the FBI to analyze the case in depth. I guess I was looking for a miracle.

It was at this point I felt a bit insulted. Here was a fellow law enforcement officer from another state who knew nothing about Lawrence or its people. This was his first time to our city, but yet he was giving us a profile of our killer without having all the pertinent information. He invited us to a meeting hundreds of miles away for several days of information exchange that we have already had since the onset of the first murder. I think not, and I made no plans to go to Quantico for idle chatter because in my mind that's how I viewed it. I meant no disrespect to the FBI, but I sincerely felt like we would be wasting valuable time by going on an information exchange in Quantico. Why not meet in Lawrence where the crimes occurred? Why not gather our information for analysis, share it with counterparts of the bureau, and then meet with us to give us direction? In no way did I possess the expertise and experience of the FBI, but I just felt I could do more at the ground level. After the meeting was over, we all shook hands and thanked him for his time. Clyde was the first to leave the room, and I left shortly thereafter where I saw Clyde outside smoking a cigarette.

"I'm not going to any damned Quantico! Is he fucking crazy?" I asked Clyde. I angrily told Clyde the killer was right in the neighborhood where the homicides took place, and I wasn't going on the trip to Quantico. I told him I was going to the chief's office to express my dismay and disappointment in the direction the investigation was headed.

I went to the chief's office where I closed the door and had a candid conversation with him. Even though I was perturbed about the FBI meeting, it behooved me to keep my feelings subdued in the chief's presence but I spoke to him in a respectful way, but in a way he knew it was all about business. The chief trusted me and trusted my instincts because he had seen me at work many times with great results. Usually, when I tell him something about my cases or ask him for something specifically, he would make sure I got what I needed. I told him I felt uncomfortable going to Quantico to discuss the case, and reiterated my thoughts of the killer being among us, and I felt like we wouldn't accomplish anything going to Quantico. I told him I wanted to work on it some more and that I had ideas I wanted to follow up on. He continuously looked down at some paperwork scattered across his desk and said, "Go to it then." It was an unusual tone he used when he spoke to me, and I felt like he was still disconnected and didn't really care what I did.

We continued to have sporadic meetings, which didn't seem to accomplish much. We did agree to split up the target list of suspects and secure a DNA sample from each. It was suggested that this practice would look like a fishing expedition or a witch hunt with no real suspect in focus. This type of so-called fishing expedition could be problematic during prosecution if not articulated correctly. I understood the likely challenges of this method, but how it looked wasn't really a factor for me as we could always justify it at a later time after we identified the killer.

CHAPTER 25

The Primary Suspects

Before we began to divide the suspects, I made it known, and I made it clear that I wanted to get Toby Singleton's sample DNA. I wanted it for several reasons. I knew Toby Singleton because I arrested him in the past. I knew his demeanor, and I knew his characteristics, and I believed he was the killer. I wanted to make sure he didn't refuse to give a sample of DNA, which he certainly would have if he was approached in the wrong way. I also wanted to question him about his whereabouts on the night of Loretta's murder.

Everyone got their assignments, and everyone was paired with a partner. I was paired with SBI Agent Sullivan. I was good with that because Sully was a hard hitter and a no-nonsense kind of guy with the old-school do-what-it-takes mentality. But he had convinced himself that Loretta's estranged husband Jeff Brodus killed her and therefore killed Sallie as well because of the likeness in patterns. Most of the pieces fit when I thought of Jeff as the killer of his estranged wife, but a few pieces just didn't add up for me.

Jeff was simply not strong enough to overtake either lady. Jeff suffered from a muscle disease, which caused him to walk with a cane and with limited mobility. I just could not fathom him struggling with these to robust and well, able-bodied women. Only if Jeff immediately incapacitated the women with a blow to the head or a fatal stab could he be capable of killing them. But there was a struggle with both victims, and either of them could have easily overtaken him or yelled for help.

I eventually took it upon myself to contact Margaret Loveton, an ex-lover of Jeff's. Margaret had moved to Fayetteville during that time, and I went to her house to get more intel about Jeff. Margaret told me she and Jeff had a tumultuous relationship, and he wasn't any good as a mate or a good father to their child. As an investigator, that bit of information was good because she would surely tell me anything that would get him locked up. So if she knew anything, I was about to find out. She told me she heard Jeff was a suspect in the homicides, but she had trouble believing he was guilty. She said Jeff's ailments were so debilitating, he could barely walk. She said he used to be a mechanic for the City of Lawrence for years until he couldn't take it anymore. He couldn't bear to bend over for extended time, and he couldn't lift heavy objects and eventually had to resign under disability. Everything she told me about Jeff confirmed my thoughts even more about him not being able to commit the murders. I needed that confirmation just to make sure I was right about Jeff and before I was completely convinced that Agent Sullivan was wrong.

Nonetheless, Agent Sullivan was convinced Brodus was the killer, and he and Detective Woodland eventually went to Brodus's house to conduct a soft-approach interview. While they were in the house, they observed a cut on Brodus's head that appeared to be healing and another old cut on one of his fingers. They also observed a pair of boots that had mud on them. Neither of them was satisfied with the interview and wanted to investigate him and his house further. In their minds, they knew Brodus was responsible for at least Loretta's death. They believed he had a motive and opportunity. They convinced themselves Brodus was not responsible for his state of mind, and they created a timeline that allowed him to commit the murder. With all these circumstantial pieces of evidence, they thought it was time to get a search warrant for his home based on probable cause they believed they had.

Both Special Agent Sullivan and Detective Woodland requested a meeting with district attorney Krystal Newman. Sullivan wanted us all to meet with DA Newman to determine if we had enough probable cause to get a search warrant for Jeff Brodus's house, which was located in rural Robeson County about forty miles from Loretta's house. As Special Agent Sullivan and Detective Woodland fed the DA incriminating and damaging information about Brodus, it appeared the information was sufficient in the DA's opinion to obtain a search warrant, and she gave them the green light.

Detective Woodland and Special Agent Sullivan procured the search warrant and went to Brodus's residence in search of any evidence that linked him to the deaths of Loretta or Sallie. They took a team of investigators and searched Brodus's house, collected the boots, and took photos of the cuts on his head and fingers. Other than that, they found nothing else.

Several days after the search was conducted, I met with the DA in her office where she was livid about our investigation of the case. She was totally pissed off that she was called to a meeting to discuss Jeff Brodus as a prime suspect but was not informed there were multiple suspects involved as well. She said she was going to meet with Special Agent Sullivan because she stuck her neck out to help us bring the case to a close but was misled to believe Jeff Brodus was the only suspect. I've known and worked with the DA for several years, and I have never seen her as upset as she was on this day. Although we all knew there were other suspects, I guess we all felt obligated to allow Detective Woodland and Agent Sullivan to follow up on their instincts, which is why none of us spoke up at the meeting to reveal the possibility of other suspects. I felt bad for not adding my two cents in the meeting because I knew Krystal trusted me, and in her eyesight, I believe she felt betrayed by me.

Since there was not enough evidence to arrest Brodus and our case was compromised because of our misguided conversations, we continued to meet and resume our partnerships. The day came when Sully and I went to Toby Singleton's apartment where he was known to reside with his sister who also knew me from Toby Singleton's previous arrest. Even though I had arrested her brother in the past, she invited us in and treated us kindly. The three of us sat in the living room where I began the conversation. I told her we were canvassing the area and asking all residents about what they knew or heard about the recent homicide. I veered off from the usual questioning because

I wanted to know where Toby Singleton was when Loretta was killed. I was as nice and subtle as I could possibly be as I told her that Toby Singleton's name had been circulating in the neighborhood as a possible suspect. I asked her if she had heard the same, and she said yes. I asked her when the last time was she had seen Toby Singleton, and she said it was about three days ago and that he usually stayed with her when he was in town. I asked her what room Toby Singleton usually sleeps in when he visits her, and she pointed to a room down the hallway that neither Sully nor I could see from our position on the couch. Little did I know that the next few moments would give me hope like I've never experienced before, and it would surely change the course of the investigation.

As I continued to ask her questions about her brother, Toby silently and with caution walked into the living room as if he was waiting around the corner and listening to every word we said. He entered the room with quiet, careful steps from one of the rooms down the hall and said, "Hey, Monroe, what's going on?" He caught me off guard because I didn't think anyone was in the apartment other than us. His sister vehemently lied to us about seeing him three days ago, which I thought was bizarre but compelling. When Toby walked in the room, he looked at me with that blank stare that I was so familiar with from the last time I arrested him for murder. I remained my calm, cool self and told him I was just asking his sister about him. I figured he heard our entire conversation, but it was time for me to put on my best nonchalant performance so I could get what I wanted, which was his DNA sample.

I made him feel comfortable as I continued to talk and smile as if it was just routine work and making him believe we were doing him a favor. I told him his name had come up several times in the investigation, and we were taking DNA samples from every suspect named. I told him if he would give me a DNA sample, we would leave him alone, and he wouldn't have to be bothered with us anymore "unless you're the one who killed Loretta," I said jokingly. He looked at me and then away as he gave a forced and fake grin as he lightly grunted.

"You didn't kill her, did you?" I asked him with a smile and still in a joking manner. He shrugged his shoulders, gave a very light chuckle, and said, "Naw," in a light tone and low volume. "So you don't mind if I get a quick sample, right?" I asked him, and again, he said, "No." I inserted the Q-tip swab in his mouth and rubbed it all around the cavity as he held his tongue out, up, and sideways. Sully and I both thanked Toby and his sister for being cooperative in such a serious case, and we left.

As we walked to our car, I looked at Sully and said, "We just interviewed the killer." Sully didn't seem quite convinced though, and he asked me if I really thought so. I said yes and asked him if he noticed Toby Singleton's demeanor, his eyes, and the fact that his sister lied for him. Sully simply said, "I don't know, Kim. I still think it could be Brodus." I said, "Okay, but that's him, that's him. I'm telling you that's him."

This was one of those times when an investigator's gut feeling gets to be overwhelming, and the body fills with excitement and anticipation. In my mind, Toby Singleton was the killer, and I could hardly wait to submit his blood sample to the laboratory for analysis. A whole new feeling came over me as I regained my confidence. I began to feel like "the man" again because I was determined and wanted to be the one who identified and nailed the killer. At least, that was my thought at the current time. We eventually sent the sample to the lab along with the others on our hit list, and the waiting game began.

CHAPTER 26

The Groundwork

By this time, most of the other investigators stopped attending the meetings to include myself. Gene Murcey and Kevon Stricklen felt like they had been shut out of the meetings because they weren't told about several meetings. They knew they had been shut out because the investigators believed they could not make a contribution. Besides, they were just narcotics officers and had no clue about major crime investigations. Little did anyone know, Gene, Kevon, and Daryl consistently gave me substantial information that led to many arrests and closed cases over the years. I've always been appreciative of their individual talents. Each one had a unique way of gathering and soliciting information and developing informants whom they would introduce to me. Gene and Kevon were real hard-nosed, hard-hitting detectives who would not stop until they got results. Those are qualities narcotics detectives must have to survive the streets of the night. Daryl, on the other hand, was a really nice guy who knew everybody in the community. Townsfolk seem to connect with him very easily and often spoke to him candidly about one thing or another when they wouldn't speak to anyone else. They called him and knew him only by the name Dal. When either of them brought me valuable information, my job would be to neatly place all the pieces of the puzzle together, make sure they connect, complete the puzzle, then package and sell it to the district attorney. How and where I got my information would seldom be discussed outside our circle, and most of my cases would either be found guilty or plea bargained after a confession.

As I sat in my office one morning, Gene and Kevon entered with a frustrated but determined look on their faces. I knew something interesting was about to happen because of Gene's look. He asked me if I really thought Toby Singleton killed Sallie and Loretta, and I said yes. Even though Clyde and Audrey were across the hall meeting with Agent Sullivan about the same case, Gene said, "Get your shit, and let's go find him. If you really feel like Toby is the one, we will get that motherfucker." He reminded me that Toby Singleton and his buddies were on the porch at the house right next door to Lorraine's the night she was killed, and that one of them had to know something. He said we were going to shake the bushes until something fell out and somebody talked. I put my papers aside, locked my office door, and the three of us hit the streets, and we hit it hard. We split up in two cars. Gene drove his blue Dodge Durango, and I rode with Kevon in his unmarked black Chevrolet Monte Carlo. Kevon and I were to look for Toby Singleton while Gene looked for anyone else who was on the porch the night of the murder like Donald Mathews or Puff Loveton. Somebody was sure to know something, and everyone who was on the porch that night was capable of doing just about anything to include murder.

It was about 2:00 PM when Kevon and I rode around in the Tara Village apartment area searching for Toby Singleton. As we slowly rode by his sister's apartment, Toby Singleton's mother emerged from the front door. We slowed down as she started walking toward our vehicle, and we parked against the curb just in front of the apartment building. I was somewhat familiar with Toby Singleton's mother, but I didn't know what she was going to do or say as she approached me on the passenger side of Kevon's car.

She politely said, "Hey, Monroe." After I responded, she asked me if we were looking for her son. I told her yes. She then startled me with her next question as she asked me in such a direct way, "Do you like my son for this murder?" I've heard the term *like* used many times on crime drama television, but I've never heard anyone use it on the streets. It was surely a first for me, but I knew she wasn't looking for bullshit conversation, so I knew I couldn't give her a bullshit answer. She may have been my only hope in capturing who I thought was the killer, her son. Besides, she did not interfere the last time I arrested Toby.

So I gave her the truth and told her yes, we were looking for Toby, and I thought he was responsible for the murder of Mrs. Brodus. It was almost as though she expected me to come by and have this conversation with her. As soon as I told her we were looking for Toby, she said she wanted to make a deal with me. She told me her son was not in the apartment at the time, but she would find him and bring him to me at the station by 6:00 PM. However, she said she would only bring him to me if I would leave him alone if I determined he was not responsible for Loretta's death. She told me to take as long as I wanted with him after she brought him to me, but she wanted him left alone after that. "You got a deal," I said, and we drove away not knowing if she would bring her son to me or not, but what did we have to lose?

In the meantime, Gene had found Donald Mathews and had already transported him to the station for questioning. We headed back to the station to assist Gene with his interview. Our mission was to tie Donald Mathews down to an ironclad statement. We wanted to know who everybody was on the porch, what time they left, why they were there, and who was familiar with Loretta. We specifically wanted to drill him about the whereabouts and actions of his cohort Toby Singleton. We watched and listened to Gene in action from an adjacent room through a one-way mirror. I wasn't sure whether Donald was just being cooperative on his own volition by giving information, or he was just giving Gene a bunch of bullshit in fear of losing his own freedom. Nonetheless, he was giving some very valuable bits of information concerning Toby Singleton, whether they were fabricated or not.

Gene and Donald had a mutual respect in the streets for each other. Donald knew Gene was a hard-nosed narcotics detective who would stop at nothing to close a case. Gene knew Donald as a drug-dealing street punk whom he had locked up in jail on a few occasions. Apparently, Donald felt comfortable talking to Gene about Toby Singleton's actions the night of the Loretta's death. He seemed so comfortable that we began to have an idea that he himself may be the killer and framing Toby Singleton in the process. Either way, Donald had a lot of valuable information that was quite convincing and compelling. We just had to decipher the lies from the truth. Sometimes, it's very difficult to tell when a person is lying, especially the criminal element, because they lie so much and so well. Even though Donald may have been lying, his statement started giving us leverage on Toby Singleton, which we desperately needed. I knew if we got enough damaging information from Donald, we could use it against Toby, which would make Toby turn against Donald. Maybe both were involved.

Donald told Gene he went to Durham to stay with friends the morning Loretta was found dead. He said he received a call from Toby Singleton about 3:00 PM, and Toby Singleton told him he had to get out of town and that he done something really bad. Donald said he kept asking Toby Singleton what he had done, but he would never say. Donald figured it was bad for Toby Singleton to call him and want to get out of town. Donald said he never returned to Lawrence to get Toby because whatever Toby did, he didn't want any part of it. Although Donald and Toby were buddies, Donald didn't want any problems with the police because he wanted to continue his criminal enterprise with as little attention and interference as possible. He knew Toby would most likely bring him that unwanted attention from the police, which he tried his best to avoid.

It started getting late, and Kevon and I walked back to my office to strategize our next plan of action.

About five minutes before six o'clock, the dispatcher informed me that Ms. Singleton and her son were waiting for me in the front lobby. Both Kevon and I looked at each other in bewilderment, uncertainty, perplexity, and pleasure. We could not believe Ms. Singleton bought her only son to the police department to be questioned in a murder case. We stood there in disbelief and in utter silence as we gathered our thoughts in our heads.

I knew Toby's mother as a hardworking, respectable woman who never had any bad connections with law enforcement. At least not to my knowledge. So, I guess I shouldn't have been surprised when she kept her word and brought Toby to the police department.

CHAPTER 27

The Confession

How were we going to approach Toby Singleton? Were we going to allow his mother in the interview room since she was the only person who could bring him in? Was Donald Mathews telling the truth about Toby Singleton's actions, or was he lying? We asked ourselves many questions within our few minutes of thought collection. Either way, we had to make a move, but the move we made toward Toby Singleton had to be great. We both knew we only had one chance to talk and question Toby Singleton, and if we blew it, we could possibly blow the biggest murder case spanning over several decades in Lawrence.

We decided to let Toby sit in the lobby for a while as we carefully watched his body language. Gene finally emerged from the interview room and gave us a quick synopsis of Donald's interview. From what we heard of the interview, coupled along with what Gene told us, we concurred in our belief that Donald was telling the truth. Kevon and I would then take that truth and systematically approach and verbally attack Toby. In our minds, he was the killer, and only he could prove to us without a doubt that he was not. If we were unsuccessful in our attempt, we had no plans on allowing him to leave the police department, and he would surely be locked up on other unrelated charges. We found an old misdemeanor warrant in our database for Toby, which allowed us to keep him in custody if he decided he wanted to leave. We never told Toby Singleton of the warrant as we wanted him to believe he was free to leave whenever he wanted. If we had served the warrant, it may have upset him, and he wouldn't want to talk to us anymore. We desperately needed him to talk, but we knew Toby would not go home this day.

We decided that I would be the first contact with Toby and his mother because of my kind personality and likeability. Kevon and I decided our offices were too small to conduct the interview, so we asked Detective Woodland to use his office. His office had much more space for multiple-seating capacity. His office was adjacent to Detective Sardoms' office where other detectives could listen, analyze, and strategize without being seen or heard via closed-circuit monitor.

Careful planning is a must when conducting serious interviews. It can sometimes take only one person in the room to be the wrong person and who could literally shut the suspect down from further conversation. One distraction could alter the criminal's thinking abilities or pattern of behavior. One wrong word could make the difference in whether the criminal talks, get angry, or think we are a bunch of idiots on a wild-goose chase. There are certainly a lot of variables we had to deal with, so we proceeded with the best techniques we had and knew.

All the detectives got in their respective places out of sight while I walked to the front lobby where Toby and his mother awaited my arrival. I greeted them both and thanked them for coming to the police department as agreed. Ms. Singleton made it very easy for me to separate her from her son when she asked me if she should stick around. I told her Toby and I had a lot to talk about, and it would be quite some time before we finished. She decided to leave but not before she gave her son a hug and kiss and told him she loved him.

Watching Toby's actions from the time he came into the police department and watching his mother's behavior before she left indicated a strong presence of guilt in my opinion. I also think deep down in her gut feelings, Ms. Singleton knew the truth. She separated from her son and departed from the building like it was the last time she was ever going to see him again as a free man. I prayed to the heavens she was right.

MONSTER EYES

I asked Toby to accompany me as we walked to Detective Woodland's office unrestrained and unrestricted. We had no physical evidence on Toby and no other real evidence other than the statement of Donald Mathews. I began the interview with just him and me in the office to develop a rapport with him. I needed to keep him calm and convince him that I was not the bad guy and that he needed to have some level of trust in me. Toby Singleton was as calm as I've ever seen him and didn't seem nervous at all, not agitated, not sweating, irritated, or intimidated. He was the classic cool-customer-type guy we studied about in our law enforcement textbooks. He could have easily fooled the untrained or the rookie officer with his behavior, but his behavior reeked and smelled of guilt in my eyesight.

As we entered Detective Woodland's office, I had Toby sit in one of two hard wooden chairs located on the left of the entrance. The chairs were closer to the exit door than where I chose to sit, but I wanted him to feel no pressure. I wanted him to know and be assured in his head that he could get up and step out of the door anytime he liked. I wanted him to think he was in control, contrary to the real game plan. As he sat in the chair, I walked past him and sat at the large matching wooden desk that faced the door. My position put a larger space than normal between Toby Singleton and me, but obviously my plan was working because I felt no resistance and no questions from him.

From the onset, I analyzed Toby Singleton, and I paid close attention to his every move, every facial expression, every body secretion, and every twitch as he sat in the chair with his legs crossed and extended. Toby knew exactly why he was summoned to the police department, and he knew he was a suspect in our murder case. But he remained unblemished, nonchalant, and somewhat disconnected as he stared at me with his piercing gray eyes. Although he managed to maintain his composure, his eyes brought me right back to what little Isaac said, "He has eyes like a monster!" His eyes and his expression gave him a deranged look that resembled a rabid animal. He continued with his legs crossed in front of him to secure and establish his composure as well as his personal space. His master plan was obviously to maintain his calm attitude to prove to us he was innocent. Little did he know his actions revealed just the opposite of what he was trying to convey.

With my pen down on the desk and my very mild-mannered and calculated caring attitude, I turned my chair toward him and began the interview by telling him about myself and my expectations. At one point during my interview introduction, I even told him I expected him to lie because that's what most people do when they are guilty and confronted by the police. I continued to tell him things about my background and my law enforcement career. After about forty-five minutes, I finished my introduction, and now it was his turn to give me some pedigree information and some background surrounding his life. It was almost like we were there only to exchange pleasantries in a schoolroom-type setting, which was exactly the environment I wanted to create. I wanted him to forget about me being the police and think of me as merely a nice guy.

Our conversation went on for several hours as we took our time talking to each other. Not only did I listen to him talking, but I followed up with a second interview, which was very similar to the first, but this time I wrote down everything he said. This type of interview style is not unusual, and the process can take anywhere from one hour to twelve hours depending upon the case at hand. The purpose of the first interview is to listen and absorb as much information as possible. It is also to determine if he was going to lie or tell the truth based on the information we already obtained from his friend Donald Mathews. Either version is considered good information from a law enforcement perspective, or in some cases, a lie is just as good as a confession. Hardly ever does a seasoned detective expose too much information or evidence about a case to the suspect. That information is purposely concealed from the suspect to allow that person to continue with his fabrication or confirm what we already knew. Compiling a bunch of lies from the suspect usually solicits bad opinions of the suspect by judges and juries and helps law enforcement to reach maximum punishment levels. Therefore, the more lies he told that we could prove was a lie, the harsher the punishment. At least, that was my hope. Most suspects don't realize that telling the truth benefits them in several ways when it comes to sentencing and punishment.

Crime drama television had poisoned the minds of many people and had landed many people in prison or death row because of their unwillingness to simply tell the truth or cooperate. I have allowed many suspects to go home after interviews, so they can say goodbye to their families and tie up loose ends when I very well could have locked them up on the same day. I've allowed suspects to go home for a couple of hours and others a couple of days knowing they would be arrested and locked up upon their return. Not many failed to return, but those who did not really suffered severe consequences behind their bad decision. Toby obviously was not one of those people that was going home, regardless of whether he told the truth or not.

It was about 10:00 PM when I began to wrap up my part of the interview with Toby. He did not confess to me and assured me he didn't have anything to do with the murder and that he didn't do it. I realized I could not get him to confess. I was disappointed and a bit bothered I could not, but I wasn't too proud to let Kevon take over the interview. As I've written previously, Kevon had his own intimidating style that some people responded to. Hopefully, he could break Toby, and we could all go home.

It was now Kevon's turn to get into Toby's head. This would be a classic case of good-cop, bad-cop role-play. We all worked so long and so well together, we understood each other's techniques and knew when to introduce the other. I offered Toby a soda and a snack from the vending machines and then excused myself from the room momentarily. I met with the other detectives, which were Gene, Clyde, Audrey, and our crime-scene investigator, Bobby Woodland. It was paramount we all worked together and listened to the interview simultaneously because we all could share useful information that could be discussed at any given moment. We were all good investigators, and it showed when all of us concurred that Toby was lying about his involvement. We all knew there was no need for him to lie if he was innocent. An innocent person can tell the truth several times over, and each story will be the same because it is the truth, and it is fact. However, a lie is usually followed up with more lies as the story continues, and people forget the lies they told. Liars change their stories, add to their stories, forget their stories, and get frustrated when they can't remember their stories.

We all stood and sat in the adjacent room listening to Kevon as he began his interview in a much more abrasive style. We were rooting for Kevon to get a home run with Toby by getting him to confess, and we anxiously awaited and watched the game as he began to mentally attack, abuse, and insult Toby. I had reminded Toby several times during my interview he was free to leave at any time, and he did not have to talk to us if he chose not to. He fully understood, yet he remained and continued to accept Kevon's verbal abuse and berating. Why on earth would an innocent man suffer such verbal abuse? Most innocent people would have gotten upset, angry, and defiant, but not Toby Singleton. He remained his same calm and cool self as Kevon got up in his face about three inches and told him he was going to rot and die in prison for the murders he committed. Kevon demanded Toby tell the truth while he still had a chance at life, but Toby calmly stood his ground and just stared at Kevon with sad eyes and that innocent, blank look he mastered ever so often and so well.

I did not want Kevon to get Toby Singleton too angry or to the point that he wanted to leave the building, so I walked back into the office and slowly calmed the atmosphere with my softer-toned voice as well as a soda for Toby. Like me, I could clearly see Kevon was getting frustrated because of Toby's demeanor and because he too was unsuccessful in getting him to confess. Before Kevon terminated his interview, he walked right in front of Toby Singleton as he sat in the chair and told him, "When they stick that needle in your fucking arm, I hope they break that motherfucker off in it. You are going to die, motherfucker. You are going to die."

As I began to speak with Toby again, I wondered what was going through his head. Was he thinking about confessing, or did he really think he had us fooled? I could not figure it out because he wouldn't let us in. His facial expressions and body language rarely changed, which made it difficult and frustrating to us. I decided in my own mind that because he had not left the building in an angry rage, he was on the brink of confessing. All we had to do was get him to talk or shed a tear, which would be the breaking point.

I began to make small talk with Toby to remind him that telling the truth could help him more than it could hurt. I began to feel like I had nothing to lose by giving him a bit of crucial information because no other technique seemed to work. I assured him we knew he killed Sallie even though we had no concrete evidence against him. I wanted to solicit some type of response from him; any response other than what he was giving us would be a breakthrough. Again, he remained calm as he shook his head from side to side and said he didn't do it. I was finished, exhausted, angry, and frustrated and decided to excuse myself from the room and allow someone else to enter.

Narcotics detective Gene Murcey was my next choice. Gene had patience and tolerance with suspects I never had. He could sit for hours talking in his monotone voice without the suspects saying anything. But after an extended time, he normally emerged from a room with a confession. I've sat in on interviews with him many times, but I hardly ever make it to the end because I get so sleepy and fidgety in hopes he would wrap it up whether he got a confession or not. Hopefully, he could work his magic and have the same effect on Toby, and the confession would come.

I walked back into the office alone as Toby sat quietly, and I began more small talk with him. Gene was directed to enter the room after about ten minutes, so Toby would not detect our plot, or as some people say, "smell a rat" among us.

Gene walked in as planned, and I introduced him. Of course, they already knew each other, but we were very careful in our approach. I remained in the office as Gene began his interview. Like me, Gene is very soft-spoken and began his interview in his pleasant and subtle voice. Gene is also short in stature, so he does not normally present an intimidating or commanding presence until he chooses his time to do so. When he does pick his time, he can be just as intimidating and as scary as anyone. He knew when to turn it on and turn it off. I never interrupted Gene's flow as he spoke with Toby, but eventually, it came a time for me to excuse myself from the office. My eyes began to get heavy as I listened to Gene's ever so monotonous style. It was going on a fifteen-hour workday for all of us, and we were steadily getting drained.

I never returned to the office, and we all waited for Gene to finish. At about twelve o'clock midnight, he emerged from the office and met us in another part of the building. I already knew the outcome based on his facial expression and absence of our high five we usually exchanged when we were victorious. However, Gene did get into a decent dialogue with Toby even though he still claimed his innocence. Just like Toby's claim of innocence never changed, neither did our thoughts about him being the killer.

Regardless of how minuscule, Gene managed to achieve a breakthrough. He got Toby to talk. Even though Toby continued to claim his innocence, he got him talking. His talking didn't amount to much, and this marked a rare occasion that Gene simply ran out of gas and had nothing left to say. Gene felt like he gave it all he had as he looked to us with a beaten face for suggestions. We were at our wit's end at this time, but we knew we couldn't give up on Sallie and Loretta. We owed it to them and their families to get closure.

We did a quick assessment of all our skills and tried to decide who would be most successful during the next interview. Our crime-scene investigator Bobby Woodland asked us if he could talk with Toby.

We all looked at each other because of the abnormality. We initially thought it was absurd, but what could it hurt? After all, he did perform the crime-scene investigation, which made him very knowledgeable of the layout of both crimes and how the women were killed. We figured Bobby could introduce and scare him with forensic science and convince him we had physical evidence to charge and convict him. Besides, there was blood in the house and a lone footprint. Maybe Toby would give Bob a sign that one of the items of evidence was his. This was Bob's first time participating in an investigative interview, but we crossed our fingers and hoped for the best.

Gene and I went back to the office where Toby Singleton was still calmly seated and introduced him to Bob. We told him what Bob's job was and that Bob had very damaging evidence against him. Bob began speaking with Toby in his normally calm and soothing voice. He politely introduced himself to Toby and told him he thought he was a good person who had done something wrong. As Bob spoke to Toby Singleton, he praised us for being dedicated, smart, and fair detectives, but reminded Toby he could only get our help if he told the truth. Bob explained to him some of the details of the evidence he collected and seductively told him about a height comparison measurement taken from the victim's stolen car. Bob got very close to Toby Singleton in an attempt to appeal to his emotion, but his tactic was not working very well. He too began to get hot and frustrated as his gray hair began to get disheveled, and his face took on a reddish tint. I must say, however, that Bob was very impressive and calculating in his approach, which was quite surprising to us.

From the looks of Toby's body language and expression, I knew it was going to be another dead end. Bob continued his interview to no avail for about an hour and finally gave up. We all left the office as I asked Toby Singleton if I could get him anything or if he wanted to step outside or go to the bathroom. He did want to go to the bathroom, and I showed him where it was. He remained unrestrained and unrestricted as he walked toward the bathroom. I made sure he remained unrestricted at all times because he was still free to leave, and we had no right or reason to keep him at the time. After he used the bathroom, I walked with him back to the office where he sat alone. Every walking second, I feared he would ask to leave, so I treated him as nice as I possibly could in hopes of him returning to the interview. Words can't express my joy as he exited the bathroom and walked back toward the office area and not toward the exit doors.

We were desperate and started giving up any hopes of a confession, but we didn't give up. Detective Clyde Sardoms had not had a turn with Toby as of yet. Clyde's demeanor is somewhat passive, and people normally viewed him as a really soft and nice guy, much nicer than I, and three times as nice as Gene and Kevon. Clyde's face, red hair, and freckles remind me of Dennis the Menace. Clyde was in fact the nicest detective out of all of us and was much softer in his approach toward suspects and criminals. He hardly ever changed his demeanor. Even when he got mad, he displayed a look of disappointment rather than anger. Honestly, I don't think I've ever seen Clyde angry to the point that it was obvious.

It was now Clyde's turn to try his baby-faced charm on Toby Singleton. Bob stayed out of the office as the rest of us returned to the office, including Detective Woodland. We sat quietly as Clyde spoke with Toby in a very caring and nurturing way. He began to move toward Toby Singleton as he continued to talk with him about the heinous crime he committed but assured him that God still loved him. He eventually got close enough to Toby where he put his hand on Toby's leg and told him to let it out. Toby Singleton never denied Clyde's accusations but continued to sit in the chair as he changed his body position several times. Readjustments of the body indicate discomfort, deception, or an attempt to hide internal feelings or to avoid emotional distress.

I was very tired at this point and maybe even delirious, but I would have bet a paycheck I saw Toby Singleton's eyes get slightly watery as Clyde spoke with him. I just hoped Clyde could break him. Clyde tried and tried but never succeeded. I knew Clyde was on the brink of a confession, but I had nothing else to offer, and neither did any of my cohorts until Toby Singleton extended his legs and crossed them in front of him again.

CHAPTER 28

The Link

At that moment, divine intervention took over and put us in a direction we thought we would never reach. The intervention was astonishing and like no other. As Detective Audrey Woodland sat on the opposite side of the room from Toby and observed him extend and cross his legs. He asked Toby, "Can you hold your foot up and let me see the bottom of your shoe?"

I'm sure the words "oh my god" went through all our minds at the same time. The boot Toby was wearing looked identical to the boot print Woodland took from the crime scene. I had studied the print very well after Bob showed me the pictures he took of it. I remembered the exact pattern of the print because it appeared to be a Timberland boot. When I looked at the bottom of Toby Singleton's boot, a nervous feeling came over me. I became excited. I so wanted to verbally attack and interrogate Toby again or at least say something to him to let him know we had him, but I had to remain calm and silent until we knew for sure he was wearing the murder boots. Besides, we didn't really know for sure because we had not verified it.

It was hard for me to remain calm, but I collected myself, calmed myself down, and politely asked him if he would mind taking off his boots and giving them to me. I made sure I asked him ever so nicely so he would not refuse. Just like he opened his mouth and gave me a saliva sample, he took his boots off and gave them to me also.

I politely told him I was going to take his boots upstairs, and I would return in just a few minutes. He agreed, and after I casually strolled out of the office, I ran upstairs still overwhelmed with excitement to Bob's office where I began talking so fast that Bob couldn't understand what I was talking about. I got my composure together and slowly said, "Bob, this is that motherfucker's shoes." Once Bob understood what I was saying, I saw Bob's face began to turn into a slight smile but not too much because Bob always remained cool even under the most adverse conditions. He knew just like I knew that those boots belonged to the killer even before he looked at the composite for comparison.

Bob looked at the composite from Loretta's house, briefly examined it, and immediately gave me a smile I rarely saw upon his face. One that almost brought us both to tears because we then knew we had the killer, and he would be charged with at least one murder of Loretta Brodus. Bob and I sat there a minute just relishing in our success after a long, hard battle we all shared. Again, I had to pull myself together before going back downstairs to confront Toby.

Now that I was sure Toby Singleton was the killer, I decided to turn the heat way up on my reapproach. I planned to turn into the vicious cop that would simply put the fear of God in his heart. I was going to reenter the room and strongly and officially accuse him of the murder. I knew I did not have to inform the other detectives of my intentions because I knew they would understand the plan and capitalize on it upon my absence after I left the room. It was to be the classic good-cop, bad-cop scenario all over again.

I went downstairs and flung the office door open so wide, it hit the wall behind it. I entered the room, looked directly at Toby Singleton with piercing eyes, and said in a hostile voice, "I got you now, motherfucker! You ain't going no nowhere tonight or ever. You killed Loretta Brodus. We got your fucking boots to prove it, and I promise you I will make sure you go to prison for the rest of your fucking life!" I then looked at the rest of the detectives, and in the same hostile voice, I said, "Read him his fucking rights!" I walked out of the office and slammed the door behind me so hard, I was surprised the tempered glass didn't break.

Now, it was time for the rest of the detectives to do their jobs, and that was to get Toby's confession. Clyde led the way again with his nice-guy approach. As Clyde spoke to him, Toby began tearing up and finally started crying as Clyde continued to console him and enticed him to let his feelings and emotions out. Clyde hugged Toby as he wept on Clyde's shoulders. I was proud of Clyde for maintaining his cool and allowing Toby to express and release what he had boxed up all day and for the last two years. Even though Toby Singleton exposed his turmoil he desperately tried to subdue, he was cautious and somewhat reluctant about talking about what he had done to Loretta. But finally, somewhere around 3:00 AM, he broke down in a midst of tears again. As Clyde continued to console him, he repeatedly spoke to him in that voice that I knew so well. No one would dare interrupt Clyde's interview because we all knew Toby was about to confess to the biggest murder the city of Lawrence has ever had.

"Let it out, let it out. It's going to be okay. God knows your heart." Those were the words Clyde echoed in Toby's ear repeatedly and ever so gently. After many of those coaxing but soothing strokes from Clyde's mouth to Toby's ears, Toby began nodding his head up and down in a positive motion and finally said, "I did it."

Still no one dared to move because it was still a moment in time where we had to continue to treat and handle Toby with the highest level of integrity while still maintaining respect toward him and as well as keeping his dignity intact despite the fact that we were looking at a cold-blooded killer.

By this time, Clyde's face was flush, and strands of hair had dropped down over his forehead as they often did upon Clyde's frustration or fatigue. We all were fatigued, but Clyde was even more so because he refused to stop interviewing when he saw a glimpse of hope. Persistence is a characteristic that only dedicated and true professionals exemplify under such pressure. Many investigators would have surely given up after such a traumatic and time-consuming fact-finding mission. It was so good knowing we all were dedicated, and all of us shared a piece of this tragic saga, which gave us the will to succeed.

Words could not have expressed the joy that overcame us all. Even Clyde took on new life as he allowed Toby to sit alone in the office and reflect upon what he had done. When Clyde exited the room, we all met in the locker room where we were very quiet as we gave each other the biggest high five ever. We stood around for a few minutes concentrating on our own inner thoughts about everything surrounding this case. It was literally just moments of silence until Clyde had to go outside to smoke a cigarette.

I experienced and embraced feelings never felt before. It was a bittersweet moment that had me choked up inside to the point I wondered what approach we would take next. I had so many emotions and so many things running through my head, I sort of lost my place in the investigation. I found myself again in an angry state of mind, cheerful, yet melancholy and bitter as well. I knew I had to put myself in check, gather my composure, and finish what we had started nine hours ago.

After about thirty minutes, Clyde and I walked back into the office where Toby sat patiently. It was my turn again, and I was to begin where Clyde left off. I began by gently asking him if he was okay and restarting the conversation by telling him that Clyde and I had a conversation about what he had done. I told him what a good job he did by telling Clyde the truth, but I didn't want him to go backward. I wanted him to continue the process and tell the truth because that was the only way we could help him. I said a few more calming words to Toby as Clyde exited the room, and I began writing as Toby gave me his account of what happened.

<u>Toby's statement was very compelling, and very forth right once he was relieved of his guilt. He told us he knew he was going to rob somebody the night he killed Loretta, but he really didn't know who it would be. Apparently, he chose Loretta's house because it was convenient and he was childhood friends with her son, Dustin. He told us that's how he managed to get into her house. When he told her his name and he was Dustin's friend, she opened the door. He said after she opened it, he stepped in and she saw the knife protruding from his coat pocket. By the time she tried to push him back out the door, it was too late. That's when he began stabbing her and striking her head with a nearby hammer. He admitted to kicking her with his boot and tying her up and dragging her about the house and into her</u>

bedroom, where he removed her clothes had his way with her after he confirmed she was no longer alive. He told us how he stole several items of jewelry, trinkets, hammer and clothing from her house that he put in a pot and placed in her car before he stole it and drove away. He took more things than he could remember.

Toby Singleton's confession took another two hours to get all of it in writing. I wrote so much information so fast, my fingers and hand began to get strained and cramped. I flexed my fingers and twisted my wrist in a circular motion in order to get to the conclusion of the written statement. After the writing was finished, I read the entire confession back to him as he sat next to me and observed the very document that would possibly send him to his death. It was his last chance to add, retract, or change anything about the confession prior to him signing his name on the dotted line. He made a couple of insignificant changes, signed his name, and dated the document. What a relief it was to see those legal pad papers filled with Toby Singleton's words of confession, but we had even more to do. As I sat and listened to Toby's confession, his eyes had a menacing effect. His eyes almost reminded me of someone who was dead. These were clearly the eyes of a monster, just like Isaac told us from the beginning.

We didn't stop there. We then handcuffed and shackled Toby to prevent any chance of escape. He knew what he had done was serious, and he could go to prison for the rest of his life or face the death penalty. We didn't want to take any chances or give him any windows of opportunities or second thoughts. Even though he gave a full confession, we needed more physical evidence to present a compelling case to the prosecutor and to a jury. We needed to convince a jury beyond the shadow of the doubt that Toby Singleton killed Loretta. He was a cold-blooded and calculated killer who would surely kill again if given the opportunity. The only reason it took him two years to kill Loretta was because he had been locked up in jail. It was only months after his release that he killed Loretta. I truly believed if he wasn't apprehended, he surely would have killed again and again.

In Toby's confession, he admitted using a knife to stab and kill Loretta. When I asked him what he did with the knife, he told us he would take us and show us where he discarded the knife after he left Loretta's house. Once Toby confessed, he became even more subdued and continued to cooperate without any provocation. It was like since he confessed, he may as well tell the whole story. Maybe he really thought we were really going to help him.

Indeed, he did. He took us to a ditch bank that sat only yards from both Loretta's and Sallie's house. He pointed to an area on the side of the ditch bank where he said he threw some of Loretta's stuff including the murder weapon. We then climbed into the ditch bank where the sounds of a small body of streaming water pierced through the early-morning hours. We found several items of ritualistic-type evidence in a plastic garbage bag just as Toby described. In the bag, we found Loretta's pants, a pot, a hairbrush, a hammer, and the knife he used to murder Loretta. It was a miracle the items were still intact. The items were lying in the brush just as Toby said, and so bizarre it was like it was meant for us to find.

It was just as I suspected. Toby had begun his life a serial killer. As noted earlier, serialists normally keep things they value from their crime scenes better known as trophies. Trophies are trinkets that are kept by the serialist that allows them to admire their work of killing or to establish a list of items from each of his victims to remind him of how many times he had killed without being caught. It can also be kept by the killer as a means of connection to his victims once they are dead. I'm sure the list goes on as to why they keep these trinkets that only a psychoanalyst could explain. Either way, it was an awry, eerie, creepy morning collecting the items as they lay in the brush after two long years.

While we were conducting the search of the ditch bank, Detective Woodland and Clyde were back at the office preparing a search warrant for Toby's residence, which was at his sister Latisha's apartment. Toby Singleton never refused or gave us any trouble after his confession, and he was forthright and accurate with most everything we asked of him. I guess he figured he didn't have anything to lose at this point. He was already at rock bottom, and the only thing he thought he could probably do was to help himself by giving information and cooperating.

It was around four o'clock in the morning when we finished collecting the evidence from the ditch bank. After we finished collecting the ditch-bank evidence, I transported him to his sister Latisha's apartment where Audrey and Clyde waited on us with a search warrant in hand. Honestly, the way things were going that morning, I don't think we even needed the search warrant. Not only was Toby being cooperative, but so was his sister after we woke her up from obviously a dead sleep. She invited us in along with her brother Toby whom she saw handcuffed and shackled. One of us read the warrant aloud to her and gave her a copy before we began searching for other items of evidence.

In her apartment, we found the same unidentified powdery-type substance we found near both Sallie's and Loretta's bodies. The matter was on the floor and right near Toby's stringless sneakers. Both victims were tied with shoestring. Miraculously, it would be the same-type string that was taken from Toby's sneakers.

Toby remained his usual calm and cool self and stood by as we collected evidence in the apartment. It didn't seem to faze him at all that we were there, and his life was about to be over as he knew it. He was probably delirious from sleep deprivation. After we gathered everything we needed, we transported him back to the police station to be booked. Then we took him to the magistrate's office where he was formally charged with first-degree murder and ordered to be held in jail without bond.

Although Toby confessed to Loretta's murder, he never confessed to Sallie's murder. But thanks to that DNA saliva sample we got from him on January 29, 2003, we were able to link him to Sallie's murder as well. We didn't need him to confess nor did we even bother to go back and speak with him about it. His DNA spoke loud and clear, and we were sure to convict him of both murders. That day could not come soon enough for all of us.

Of course, Toby was indigent and could not afford legal representation, so he was eventually provided a team of attorneys that attempted to prepare and build a case to defend him. After two more years of jostling between the district attorney's office and the defense counsel, his attorneys offered a plea bargain of which the district attorney and all of us gladly accepted. Even though there were a few potentially problematic errors within the case, I'm sure the defense knew they had a slim chance of winning their case with a jury. The defense also knew if their client plead not guilty but was found guilty, he would also face the possibility of being put to death.

Toby Singleton agreed to a plea arrangement of three life sentences without chance of parole. He would serve the rest of his life in prison and will eventually die there. Unfortunately, the death he would face would be of no comparison to the brutal death he brought upon Sallie and Loretta. He is currently serving his life sentences in maximum confinement in a North Carolina prison. His family still resides peacefully somewhere in the town of Lawrence.

I left several life-altering facts about Toby out of the book in hopes that I will be encouraged and inspired to write another one. One of the interesting things I found out about Toby was that he was sexually molested as a child, which he ultimately carried throughout his life. Not only did it seem to affect him mentally, but physically as well. We had a chance to speak to a few of his former girlfriends who told us Toby had problems with intimacy, and he was sexually dysfunctional. Maybe this was the reason for his internal rage, but only Toby knows for sure.

Sometimes I wonder who would have been next and how long would it have taken for him to take another life. I wondered when, why, and what triggered him to become the gray-eyed monster he became. These are questions only Toby himself can answer, and maybe one day he will. His rage, his anger, fears, and inferiorities are obviously emotions and behaviors that deserve research not only for his sake, but for the sake of other innocent people who may die by the hands of the same type of deviant behavior. A few months after Toby's arrest, Lorraine Freeman paid me another visit at my office. Lorraine was the sister of Charles Freeman, the man who was tragically beaten by Singleton and his cohorts several years ago. She wanted to thank us for a job well done, and for not giving up on the women who were murdered and her brother Charles. She said in her angelic voice, "Remember, I told you everybody who took part in the killing of my brother would be brought to justice? Justice has prevailed. Every one of those boys has been locked up and some are even still doing time. I never wish any harm to anybody, but those boys deserved what they got, and I just want to thank you." We embraced for a moment, and she left never to be seen again.

This is a case I will never forget as long as I live. By the time this book is hopefully published, I will most likely be retired and living somewhere else where I can reflect peacefully upon all the good things we've done as a team and what I've done throughout my career to assist in bringing criminals to justice in the beautiful state of North Carolina.

CPSIA information can be obtained
at www.ICGtesting.com
Printed in the USA
LVHW110229040220
645650LV00001BA/189